for
Junaydah, Jamal & Makaela
(and their phenomenal parents)

Contents

Gifted At Primary, Failing By Secondary

Neil Mayers

Gifted At Primary, Failing By Secondary

Published by ill-Literation
PO Box 62506
London

ISBN 0955 55942 6

EAN 978-0-9555594-2-6

Typeset by Darkeye Images

Cover design by Darkeye Images

Introduction

I often ask schoolchildren to explain what they think is the purpose of a bank. By far the most common response is, "To look after your money". I quickly respond by asking if they really think that a bank's only purpose is to provide a public service. Do rich individuals or groups of rich individuals build banks to serve the community or to serve themselves? After realising that the supposedly obvious is now making little sense, it doesn't take long for them to realise that the true purpose of a bank is to make money using other people's money. Most people are a lot less accommodating of institutions that are designed to exploit them.

Similarly, parents of children of African descent in Britain must realise the purpose of a British school. Its purpose is not to educate.

The purpose of state schools has not changed in England since the 60's and 70's when there was a huge demand for factory workers for the country's economic development. The purpose of a British school is to create a stock of good British subjects. That is, to create 'worker-bees' that will serve this country well, and keep the wealth in the hands of those who have it now. By implication this also means keeping things the way they are, which unfortunately for most people of African descent means remaining on the bottom rungs of society be it in terms of race, class, economics or a combination of the three.

If you are British*, then the negative impact of this education system will be minimised. This is not to say that there will *not* be a negative impact because as it stands, the British education system is not even doing European people any favours. At least as a European, a British education will not cause any cultural damage to the individual. However, if you are of African descent you must rapidly come to an awareness that putting your child through the education system in this country is going to cause some degree of psychological damage (as will be discussed in the course of this book). As a parent, you will spend a great deal of your time trying to reverse or minimise the effects of that damage. This *is* a manageable task. Unfortunately, as a parent you also have the

---

* By this I mean a White individual whose parents, grandparents, great grandparents etc. were born and raised in the UK. Not simply those carry a British passport.

vi

unenviable task of trying to educate your child on: the effects of media stereo-typing; institutionalised racism; sexual health in an increasingly sexualised soci-ety; negative peer pressure (remember, all peer pressure is not negative); drug awareness; violence amongst our youth; sexism; ageism; classism and the list goes on. Do not forget that you also have to ensure your child has a strong cul-tural identity through knowing themselves and their African and Caribbean histo-ry. That'll keep you pretty busy! And if you're a single parent, it's a wonder if you can manage half of that whilst putting food on the table and paying all the bills.

Although its impact cannot be ignored, this book does not assume to deal with the reasons why the British education system as a whole has such a profoundly negative impact on African and Caribbean children. This question has already been expertly handled in books such as:

HOW THE WEST INDIAN CHILD IS MADE EDUCATIONALLY SUB-NORMAL IN THE BRITISH SCHOOL SYSTEM: The Scandal Of The Black Child In Schools In Britain, Bernard Coard

TELL IT LIKE IT IS: How Our Schools Fail Black Children, Brian Richardson

It has also been discussed in:

THE RAMPTON REPORT (1981): Enquiry into the education of children from ethnic minority groups.

THE SWANN REPORT (1985): Enquiry into the education of children from ethnic minority groups.

This book attempts to answer a question that thousands of parents have asked after their child has spent some time in an English secondary school,

Why are they doing so badly now they are in secondary school when they did so well at primary school?

There are a lot of positive things that happen whilst the child is at primary school. In the course of this book some of these things will be highlighted and contrasted with their lives at secondary school. Although there are many instances where the question is raised, "If it was working at primary level, why change it at secondary?" the intention is not to give the impression that primary school education is perfect. However, there are numerous models of good educational practice that parents are familiar with that occur in most primary schools. For that reason it was convenient to use these common practices as examples.

Additionally, attitudes and behaviours of both children and their parents change after the transition to secondary school. In some cases, a number of these changes in behaviour appear to be the result of unconscious decisions. Nonetheless, whether intentional or not, these changes as well as their effects are scrutinised and solutions offered to maximise the academic achievement of the child whilst they attend secondary school.

This book does not claim to have every answer that you need to solve every problem. However, there is a wealth of answers here for parents that can be quickly digested and made part of everyday life so that at least educationally, the battle is not a lost cause. More importantly, this book will help to ensure the beautiful, talented and confident individual that left primary school in Year 6 does not become a frustrated, apathetic and jaded shadow of their former selves by the time they leave secondary school in Year 11.

Part 1

Exposing

Some Myths

That's Racist!
How?
I don't know!

Racism Is Not The Same As Racial Prejudice

A lot of us take it for granted that if we are Black then we must know what we are talking about when it comes to racism, but this is simply not the case. Having spent a fair amount of time in the US, I quickly became aware of the intensity of racism especially towards people of African descent <u>in the UK</u> which was only made stronger by its apparent absence. I remember a quote from the film The Usual Suspects, "The best trick the devil ever played on the world was to make them believe that he didn't exist." This is an excellent analogy for the pattern of majority of racism in the UK. Racism in the UK is hardly ever in your face.

My first real 'light-bulb' moment was after my first trip to the USA when I was nine years old. I was overwhelmed by the number of television channels. I loved the sitcoms that had African-American families such as **Good Times, Cosby Show**, and **The Jeffersons**. A lot of these sitcoms showed families dealing with cultural issues and finding solutions as a family, and these shows all received the highest ratings and viewer figures, and they aired in or around the 'Prime-Time' slots. It was only after my return to London that I realised what the Black community in the UK was missing. There was only one show that centred around a Black family – **Desmonds**. Almost three decades later, the UK has been introduced to satellite and cable television. There are now nearly a hundred channels, but there is now (August 2008) a grand total of **<u>zero</u>** British-made television shows centred around Black families! I often challenge my students to name

2

a television programme that even contains a long-standing Black couple. The question is usually followed by silence or embarrassed laughter.

Because most children have never known any better some say that they have not seen any racism. That is because they have yet to learn how to use their eyes properly. Unfortunately, because there are many adults who also claim that they have not experienced racism, this gives some less conscious people the impression that racism does not exist. It could easily be argued, *that* is the proof that racism in the UK is working almost perfectly!

'Race', 'Racial Prejudice', 'Racism', 'Racist', 'Racial Abuse', 'Institutionalised Racism'…

These are words and phrases that are thrown around so much that often they are used without a full understanding of exactly what they are.

Racism (and all of these related terms) is based on **race**. Therefore it is important to know what 'race' is and what the different races are.

This creates the first and most significant problem. There is no *scientific* definition for race, because race is not a scientific concept. Race is a *social* concept. What is meant by 'race is a social concept'? Well, 'race' was first used for a reason. It was used by Europeans, for Europeans to describe the differences between the different people they were meeting as they explored the rest of the world.

Different people traditionally have different ways of dealing with unfamiliar cultures and groups. Africans are generally very welcoming. The Chinese and Japanese are generally very guarded. English traditions suggest that when exploring new lands and encountering the residents, the common reaction is not to build relationships or keep them at 'arms length' but rather to conquer and completely obliterate the population. Obvious examples of this behaviour would be the genocide of the Native Americans (often referred to as Red Indians), the genocide of the Native Australians (often referred to as Aborigines), and the multiple genocides of Africans in different countries on the African continent and worldwide.

3

In fact, on their own shores the English have tried to wipe out the Scottish, Welsh and some of the older generations in England may remember shops signs that read, "No Dogs, No Blacks and No Irish".

Historically, bogus definitions of race have repeatedly been used by to justify the immoral treatment of light-skinned people over dark-skinned people. Today, the same tactics are still being used by western nations to fuel wars in less economically developed countries. For example the Belgians used the social grouping of *class* in Rwanda – Tutsis and Hutus, turned it into a scientific classification of *race*, set the two groups against each other using the divisive, but familiar tactics of promoting 'democracy', then supplied arms while the warring groups killed each other.

Distinct classifications of race are even more difficult to understand when we keep in mind that the entire human race are descendants of Africans. Africans have dominant genes whilst Caucasians have recessive genes, which means that it is biologically impossible for all of the branches of the human family (Africans, Asians, Chinese, Europeans etc.) to have come from a non-African root.

Because of this lack of clarity in definitions, it is understandable why foolish debates take place where the Irish people claim they experience racism from the English (even when they are both Caucasian), or where Jews are identified as a race when Judaism is a religion.

For the purpose of moving the discussion towards a conclusion, 'Race' is defined here as:

the semi-scientific classification of human beings into groups identified by their recent (last 5,000 years) continent or region of origin.

Therefore, racial prejudice is defined as:

the discrimination of one person or group on another, based on their race.

Racial abuse is then:

the ill-treatment of a person or group as a result of racial discrimination.

4

Racism however describes a much bigger arena than individual prejudice.

Racism is racial discrimination on a global scale.

This is where the schools, colleges, universities, media, entertainment industry, fashion industry, police, military and all aspects of society support and promotes the belief that one race is inherently superior or inferior to the others.

Therefore,

a racist is an individual who not only subscribes to the belief that one race is inherently superior or inferior to the others, but one who can identify with the group that has the power to implement that belief into every aspect of society.

Consequently, a Nigerian man hurling abuse at a Scottish man because of his origin is not a racist because he is not a part of that power structure. He is however, being racially prejudice.

It is important that as parents we understand the difference between racism and racial prejudice, because the media would have you believe that they are interchangeable terms that mean exactly the same thing. Furthermore, the media promote the philosophy that *anybody* can be racist and at times we are all equally guilty of racism. That is simply not true. One arena is vastly different to the other.

Additionally, we must recognise and take responsibility for immersing our children into such a hostile environment as a UK state school. To submit a child to such a historically racist institution without the cultural safety net of '**knowledge of self**' is negligence in the extreme.

Beware of Useless Examinations

Think about these 2 questions:

1. After students left school, did any employers, college administrators or university administrators ask for SAT* results?

Answer: No!

2. If SAT examinations carried any value, why didn't Independent Schools make their students sit them?

Answer: Because they were worthless!

SAT examinations came into effect during Margaret Thatcher's Conservative party administration in the 1980's. They were launched quite skillfully. The idea was first to introduce standardised tests then, print the results of each school for everyone to see (league tables). The schools with the lowest results would have to be assessed to determine if the teaching and learning was up to standard. Naturally, that would require a department whose job was to assess the quality of schools (OFSTED†). The so called 'failing' schools would then be prime targets for privatisation, the logic being that a failing school would need a cash injection and support from the community.

---

*　Standard Assessment Tests, also called National Curriculum Tests
†　Office of Standards in Education

Ultimately, it was hoped that the annual financial burden of educating the children of this country would not have to fall to the government. This would allow them to spend that money on more important items (such as weapons).

The whole plan was skilfully sold to parents.

1. OFSTED was the best way to measure quality of a school and the competence of its staff;
2. League tables were the best way to compare schools when deciding the most appropriate place for your child to receive their secondary education; and
3. SATs were sold as the best way of measuring progress and making sure that your child was 'on-track'.

1.   OFSTED

The effectiveness of OFSTED is discussed in the next chapter.

2.   League Tables

League tables (and SATs) have been boycotted in Scotland and Wales, attacked by every teaching union, and criticised by most teachers* for numerous reasons:

a) By focusing on results which are printed in league tables, students are taught to do well in the tests rather than taught to be prepared for the world of work or further education.

b) League tables are misleading. They treat subjects and schools as if they are equal, not taking into consideration the hours allocated for each subject, the ethos of the school, the student intake, the location of the school (rich/poor area) etc.

c) The existence of league tables results in unfair teaching practices. Those students who are considered borderline level 5, or borderline grade C

---

* Even the Head teacher at Eton College chose to opt out of the league tables for independent schools in 2008

often have a lot more time, money and effort directed at them because converting *their* grades can significantly affect the school's overall pass percentage and subsequent league table standing. Strong students and weak students are often left to their own devices because minor changes in *their* grades will not significantly affect the schools results.

Not long after the first publication of this book, SAT examinations were abolished in England so the chapter seemed pointless. However, after the removal of the SAT examinations it quickly became obvious that a lot of work had already been done to create a replacement – Functional Skills Tests.

Functional Skills had an almost flawless marketing scheme:

- Britain had fallen behind other industrialised nations across the world. It's children needed an education system that was up to date.
- Employers across the country were complaining that the education children are currently receiving has been 'dumbed-down'. Eleven Plus' Exams that employers sat before they started secondary school were more challenging than the GCSE examinations that year eleven students take when they are 16 years-old!
- Educators had commented on subjects being taught in isolation – having little or nothing to do with other subjects being taught across the curriculum.
- Parents also complained that the current education system did not equip students with the skills they needed to succeed in the 'real world'.

Lo and behold the saviour of British Education – Functional Skills!

However, those responsible for introducing Functional Skills also recommended that no child should be permitted to receive a GCSE grade from A* to C UNLESS they had passed their Functional Skills examinations! Do not skip lightly past that last sentence. Take the time to read it over again. If that recommendation had not been rejected, the functional skills examinations would literally have become the "gate-keeper" for further education. Effectively, they would have become more important than any GCSE examination because you could not obtain any top grade GCSEs without them.

Make no mistake that if functional skills had been introduced in its original form, schools would have quickly realised that they had to pump huge sums of money into making sure that their students passed their Functional Skills exams. Consultants would have been paid ridiculous wages by Local Education Authorities to guarantee their students had every 'opportunity' to maximise their GCSE grades. The Department of Functional Skills would have expanded at a extraordinary rate to manage the demand for 'experts' to assess their Functional Skills Standards.

To ease the minds of the parents and help them select the correct school for their children, schools' Functional Skills results would have been published in national newspapers. Does any of this sound familiar?

Even if you do not recognise this pattern, I am sure that you can imagine the vast sums of money that hinged on the decision to link Functional Skills exams to GCSE 'passing' grades. You may wonder why I have bothered to mention something which did not even happen. The reason I spent time explaining this scenario is very important for understanding the motives of those in charge of educating our children. Almost every element of British society has recognised how ineffective they current education system is. Faced with this problem, the choice was not made to give the education system a complete overhaul (as has been done in numerous countries). Instead, an opportunity was seen to make minor 'tweaks' to the education system then, make a hell of a lot of money 'managing' those changes.

There is a global myth that a British Education is the best in the world. Meanwhile, students from almost every other part of the globe can step into a British school and academically put their peers to shame. It is only a matter of time before this myth is exposed on a global scale. What will follow will be a nationwide audit of British education and a national realisation that the current British education is actually one of the worst in the world. Then we will all have to send our children home for a good education!

It didn't happen this time, but beware of any national exams that are not used directly as entrance requirements for college.

There's nothing worse than tests. I'm not talking about testing and monitoring *students*. I'm talking about the testing of teachers!

From the government's point of view however, there is nothing more useful to keep teachers preoccupied than the threat of an impending test. Failure of which will guarantee that every teacher's workload will be doubled at the very least. Although the results of OFSTED inspections can be a useful gauge of the quality of teaching and learning in a school, they work on major assumptions which do not hold much weight when scrutinised. Ask any OFSTED inspector if it is possible for a teacher to get failing grades for all their students but receive a mark of OUTSTANDING in an OFSTED inspection. You might hear a fudged reply but the bottom line is that they can. Similarly, a teacher whose students consistently exceed their expected grades can repeatedly receive a judgement of 'unsatisfactory teaching' from OFSTED inspectors. How is this possible? Simple, a judgement has been made that there are only certain ways to ensure that students are learning. All evaluations are based on that. So a teacher who drills his students on the periodic table will fail an inspection. Keep in mind that an OFSTED inspection is essentially an interview. You are supposed to show the interviewer the **best** of your teaching skills. So it *is* an act. But what kind of assessment does not take into consideration a past record. Even in an interview the person behind the desk can look at a CV or contact a referee. This lack of thorough assessment betrays its true intentions – to keep you pandering to the system rather than challenging it.

Like wars, there is a lot of money to be made in 'putting things right'.

Perhaps you are a parent of a child in a school that is under *'Notice To Improve'*. Or you have past experience of a school that has been deemed a *failing* school, or *at risk* of failing. Did you notice how much money was then pumped into that school? Did you notice how many consultants began showing up? Did you notice that there seemed to be a lot of new 'Assistant Head teachers' (requiring huge salaries) all of a sudden? Did you notice the new initiatives and new projects that came with this new regime?

With glowing reports from OFSTED certain funds are more accessible. With more cash to play with, better and/or more experienced teachers can be employed. Better teachers mean better learning, which means better grades, which means higher ranks on those divisive league tables. That means that you can choose a better intake of Year 7 students from the waiting list – not those refugees, Special Needs students or EAL* students who bring down the percentages. Better intake means better performance next year so we can select a better intake the year after (even though these schools are not officially 'selective' schools). Better results mean better OFSTED reports, and the cycle continues...

---

*   English as an Additional Language (EAL)students often bring down exam percentages for
the simple reason that you need to be fluent in English to be able to read the questions and/
or write the answers.

You've Been Trained To Sell Out, And Your Children Are Next!

Nobody wants to admit to this. Why should you? It's embarrassing!

Those educated in the UK are a little more accepting of the effects of institutionalised racism. However, some people truly believe that being educated in the Caribbean or on the continent of Africa somehow makes you exempt from the devastating effects of colonial education. This may stem from the belief that it is impossible to act 'White' if there are no White people around. This is called 'living in denial'.

Here are some examples of living in denial:

Expectation / Wish / Hope	Reality
If you think your husband really heard you when when he replied, "Yeah!" while he was watching football...	...you are living in denial
If you think the 'terrible twos' is as bad as it gets...	...you are living in denial
If you think your wife will put your cds/dvds back in the right cases after playing them...	...you are living in denial
If you think that being educated in Africa or the Caribbean means that you avoided a colonial education...	...you are living in denial

Colonial education is the education that would have been received by every African on the continent or in the Caribbean since at least the 1930's. Whether from an English, French, Dutch, Belgian, Spanish or German colony, this education would have been first from the missionaries before being 'improved' upon (following careful study of the potential for mental enslavement) by the government of the colonial power itself.

In *How Europe Underdeveloped Africa*, Walter Rodney describes colonial education:

"It was not an education system that grew out of the African environment or one that was designed to promote the most rational use of material and social resources. It was not an education system designed to give young people confidence and pride as members of African societies, but one which sought to instil a sense of deference towards all that was European and capitalist.

...and to make matters worse the racism and cultural boastfulness harboured by capitalism were also included in the package of colonial education. Colonial schooling was education for subordination, exploitation, the creation of mental confusion and the development of underdevelopment."

p.262, Walter Rodney, 1989

Today, this education system still has not taught Africans at home or in the Diaspora how to rid themselves of their debts to the World Bank, or how to create wealth that can be held within the borders of their own 'independent' nations. It still teaches children to place the USA and UK on pedestals and look down upon traditional African values and practices. The most 'educated' Africans and Caribbeans still manage to siphon the riches of Africa away from its own shores to Western countries for the betterment of their economies and the detriment of their own. Hospitals perform blood transfusions, but schools perform cultural identity transfusions as Africans on the continent and in the Diaspora are made to believe that they are English first, or French first, or Belgian first etc. and African last.

In the 1920's Governor Cameron of then British-owned Tanzania (then called Tanganyika) was **attacked** by the British government for "trying to preserve

13

the African personality in the educational system". That's quite a while before the colonial education system was really at its most 'effective'.

The agenda has always been clear. If you become a successful leader in our community, be aware that it has been *despite* the education system, not because of it. To believe that you have not been affected by this huge, psychological 'machinery' designed specifically for us, requires an equally huge level of arrogance and self-denial.

Part 2

Why They Suceed In Primary

Regular Parental Involvement

Do you remember your child's first day of primary school? It was probably more traumatic for you than it was for them. And why shouldn't it be? The first day of letting go of your child into a serious schooling system. The first day of a long journey through education which lasts a minimum of eleven years. Not surprisingly, parents want to know:

- Who their teacher is going to be?
- What is that teacher like?
- How long have they been teaching?
- What do other students, parents and teachers think of this teacher?
- Who can vouch for this teacher (references)?
- Do they know all of their child's likes / dislikes / allergies etc.
- What will their classroom look like?
- Who will my child be sitting next to?
- What are the other children in that class like?

And the list goes on!

Why?

Because it takes a lot to put the most precious person in your life in the care of someone else. Consequently, any parent in their right mind is going to make sure that the people and the environment that will be a major part of their child's life from now on <u>are safe</u>. Furthermore, they will want to be sure that their child is not just safe, but that their new environment is going to be beneficial to their growth as an individual.

But that is still not enough. These parents will make sure that everyone who works in the school has their contact details. Furthermore, these parents will have gained assurances that if anything unusual happens to their child that they should be notified immediately. Over the course of the year, the parents get to know the school, the Head teacher, their child's teacher, the teacher who will be looking after the child the following year, the other students and the parents of the other students – on a first name basis.

Every day these parents ask their child how they found school and what happened that day. Each day the child is happy to provide a full report of what happened (often with a demonstrations), with whom, and with some indication of how enjoyable or disagreeable each element of the day was <u>with reasons</u>.

Days of…

Parent:	"How was school?"
Child:	"Fine"
Parent:	"What did you do?"
Child:	"Not much"
Parent:	"Did you get any homework?"
Child:	"No"

…seem an unthinkable future. And so they should!

Look at the process that most large corporations use to ensure they are progressing efficiently and all but guarantee their success.

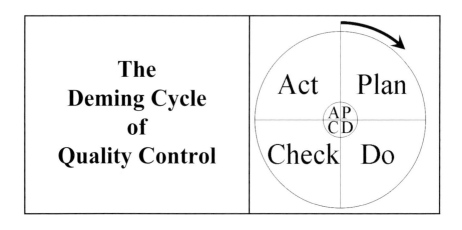

PLAN
Establish the objectives and methods to deliver the best results.

DO
Implement the necessary methods.

CHECK
Monitor and evaluate the methods used and the results against the original objectives, then report the outcome.

ACT
Apply actions to the outcome for necessary improvement. This means reviewing all steps (Plan, Do, Check, Act) and modifying the method to improve it before its next implementation.

Now look at what parental involvement occurs naturally for primary school children. You may notice the similarities in procedure.

- A critical assessment of the school usually at least a year before their child's entry. This assessment at the very least will consist of asking other parents what they think of that primary school.

- A critical assessment of the staff of the school that will come into contact with your child.
- An assessment of the learning environment of your child (the classroom).
- An assessment of the schools administrative procedures. N.B. If parents are not satisfied with the procedures in place to contact them, most parents do not have a problem with instructing the school to change their procedures to suit their needs (e.g. I want you to keep ringing me until you get through).
- A review with their child for every single day of their learning. This process itself is the most valuable part of learning – reviewing and evaluating what has been imparted to your child, as it will demonstrate to the parent whether the information they received was understood.
- An evaluation with their child. If something did not go according to plan, the parent and child discuss a way to improve the situation next time.
- A monitoring process is created. Either the parent asks how things are going, or requests that their teacher keep an eye on them for the next few days, or the parents themselves ask for support from the other parents who all monitor the situation as well.

With all this support it's a wonder how any child can fail!

Summary
Why They Succeed In Primary: Regular Parental Involvement
• Pre-assess schools, their ethos, their staff and administrative procedures • Assess your child's learning environment • Review and evaluate each day's learning • Make necessary improvements and ensure changes are monitored   and re-evaluated.

Peer pressure is defined here as:

"Pressure from one's peers to behave in a manner similar or acceptable to them."

When we talk about peer pressure it is often in the context of being with teenagers and usually detrimental to their well-being. But peer pressure does not have to be bad. Teenagers already put pressure on each other and themselves regarding appearance, personal hygiene and debating. In sports students often encourage each other to practice. Even in class, students often try to show off their intellectual strength by asking questions they hope even their teachers will not be able to answer!

In primary school, students still want to receive as much praise as possible and will try hard to obtain that praise from their 'daytime parent' (teacher). This means correctly answering as many questions as possible, being as helpful to the teacher as possible and being equipped to succeed in as many activities as possible. This could range from having the most coloured pens for art, to learning the multiplication tables early so that they are the best in the class at mathematics. Upon seeing a student like this, the pressure is on for other students to improve and often engage in more practice of: a musical instrument; a particular sport or reading to be better at something than the rest of the class. These young students often harass their parents for a better pencil case, calculator, set of paints or membership to an after-school club to improve their skills. This is the kind of peer-pressure we hope our children conform to.

Let's remind ourselves of the usual classroom setup in most African countries and in the Caribbean. Through many conversations and personal experiences, the classroom arrangement in African schools is generally one where the most successful student sits at the front of the class (having earned that position), and the least successful student sits at the back of the class. However demeaning you may think that classroom setup is, understand that every student in that class is trying their best to work their way to the front of the class. The back of the class is not a position of prestige. Rather, it is a position that will almost assuredly come with a degree of exclusion from the rest of the class. This is because the peer pressure the student is exposed to is one which values education, respects the authority of the teacher and has the expectation that each student will try their best to achieve the best possible grades.

At primary school age, creating or maintaining positive peer pressure is a fairly simple process. As a parent you simply do not allow your child to have 'sleepovers' with disreputable children – be they friends from school or unsavoury cousins or friends of family. Furthermore, when parents hear of exceptional children at school or in the family, most parents (as long as they are on reasonable terms with the child's parents) will make an effort to get their child acquainted with a peer whose positive attributes will 'rub-off' onto their own child. In an adult world this is simply known as 'networking'.

Overly liberal-minded people will label this behaviour by parents as 'choosing your children's friends for them'. This equates to some form of 'slavery' if their child is not free to choose their own friends. To those people I can only wish them all the best of luck (which I do not believe in) as they battle their way through the terrible twos and threes, the appalling fours, the frightful fives and terrifying teenage years until they are mercifully allowed to die after their disgusting children leave home. For everyone else with a drop of common sense, they will (and should continue to) surround their children with people of all ages who will feed and nurture their spirit in a positive manner.

21

Additionally, as well as your run-of-the-mill activities such as football, netball, swimming and athletics, find a way to get your child involved in less common activities.

The sooner your child becomes comfortable with standing out from the crowd (for positive reasons) the easier it will be for your child to confidently excel by the time they reach secondary school rather than fear standing out as an exceptional student.

Summary

Why They Succeed In Primary: Positive Peer Pressure
• Identify parents and classmates who have positive attitudes about their academics, their hobbies and themselves. • Identify children who engage in diverse activities e.g. chess or fencing rather than just football or netball. • Make sure that these individuals maintain contact with your children by play-dates, sleepovers or project work.

High Teacher Expectations

There is something that a primary school teacher can feel that secondary school teachers and college/university lecturers only ever catch a glimpse of in its purest form. That is, feeling that you are significantly helping to shape the positive character of a human being.

A primary school teacher often sees a negative behaviour in a child (perhaps to one of their peers), but after a few words of correction and a few more words of encouragement can resolve the situation by ensuring apologies are given, accepted and after a big hug, the children can resume their activities in an unresentful frame of mind. Not only that, but the primary school teacher can often successfully use that incident to remind the child how to resolve similar situations that arise. Secondary school teachers *do* experience similar issues. However, there is always the knowledge in the back of their mind that one of their well-behaved students *could* be making it very difficult for other members of staff elsewhere in the school.

In that respect, the primary school teacher, who spends a great deal of the children's waking hours shaping and developing their learning, has a real sense of limitless expectation of each child's potential for growth. Growth in respect to academic achievement but more importantly, in social and emotional growth.

23

Additionally, we must not ignore 3 very powerful factors that shape the way primary school teachers interact with their students:

1.   Nurturing instinct of female teachers;
2.   Cuteness; and
3.   Size.

More than 90% of primary school teachers are female. When around very young children, female teachers often cannot help but act in a maternal, nurturing manner. That is ideal for a young learner, especially when in the care of their 'daytime parent' (full-time primary school teacher).

Cuteness is not all positive. It can have its benefits and detriments. If a teacher thinks a child is so cute that they could not possibly do anything wrong the pros and cons are clear. The positive affect is that the child has someone who has unconditional faith in their character. This type of support is essential in the child's development of self esteem. The negative affect is that the child comes to realise that they can get away with almost anything. This *lack* of support will serious retard their spiritual and moral growth.

Additionally, the source of this feeling of cuteness must be addressed. There are still strong remnants of the colonial mentality which has White women adopting Black babies as extravagent 'toys' or exotic 'pets'. The image shown opposite was not unusual around the 18th Century. Look at how the pose of the little African child is one showing awe as well as loyalty to the adult. Superstars such as Angelina Jolie and Madonna's 'adoptions of many colours' is an example of there being a little more at work than just hospitality.

The point is, even high expectations can be challenged if the source of those expectations is prejudiced. For example, a discussion around a particular European child could mention their Level 5 **ability** whereas the discussions for a similar African child could mention how they produced Level 5 **work**. A parent that heard the latter might not pick up on the wording used. The language used is slightly different but the implications are hugely different. The first implies that you are dealing with a level 5 child – in **any** subject area. The second however states only that **work** has been produced at Level 5.

Even a level 3 student could produce a level 5 piece of work once in a while but they will not be called a 'level 5 student' because the teacher may not believe that level can be achieved consistently across most topic areas. It leaves more room for manoeuvre by the teacher if they feel that a child was 'boxing above their weight'. Listen carefully to the language used for your child. Listen specifically to what is being stated as fact and what is being implied. This will help you gain an understanding of the teacher's expectations of your child.

Summary

Why They Succeed In Primary: High Teacher Expectations
• Primary school teachers feel as though they are 'shaping' a young individual • Feeling of unlimited potential with each young individual. • Cuteness acts positively in the children's favour at that age • Must be careful of cuteness being literally associated with being a teacher's 'pet'

As a secondary school teacher who has visited a number of primary schools for professional development training one thing is certain, we have a great deal of admiration and respect for primary school teachers. We wonder how they remain so positive all day, every day with children in constant need of attention running around their knees at 100 miles per hour. The positive energy that can be felt in each classroom is astounding (in comparison to an average secondary school). This is a reflection of the manner in which the children learn, how conflicts are resolved and how the children work to actively support their peers (it's not often that you see a <u>Year 11</u> class applaud a good answer or presentation without a prompt from a teacher!)

A supportive, nurturing and safe environment is one of the most important factors of your child's achievement, and one of the main reasons they have achieved such a high level of success by the end of primary school. Time is taken to praise the children. Time is taken to correct negative behaviour <u>with love</u>. Time is taken to support the students when struggling with work noticeably, with the <u>absence</u> of any humiliation. Time is taken to encourage the students to reach for higher goals by everyone in their immediate environment, which is later reinforced when they reach home.

Another important aspect of primary schools is the method of discipline. Especially at a young age, children's behaviour is managed by clear explanations of what is morally and ethically right and wrong. There is a great deal of emphasis placed on empathising with a student or teacher that has been wronged. The student receives emotional and spiritual gratification as reward for their positive behaviour. Consequences are often in the form of social exclusion or removal of privileges. Unfortunately, there has been a significant increase in the use of exclusions with Black children, even at primary school age. However, this is far from being the most common method of disciplinary measure in school.

Summary

Why They Succeed In Primary: Nurturing & Morals

- Students congratulating other students on good work is the norm
- A lot of praise is given
- Positive behaviour is rewarded
- Conflicts are usually resolved using 'restorative justice techniques (where the aggressor is taught to put themselves in the shoes of their victim)

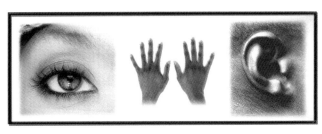

Recognition And Teaching To Different Learning Styles

For those unfamiliar with the theories of Learning Styles, they are given below:

Visual Learners:

learn through seeing...

A visual learner is someone who learns best by using their eyes to see information. They learn best by seeing words and numbers printed in text form, or by using graphics and pictures, observing real life objects and events, using maps, charts, graphs, and other visual aids.

Auditory Learners:

learn through listening...

An auditory learner is someone who learns best by listening and talking. They take in information best by their sense of hearing. They learn reading and other subjects by listening to someone present information orally and by being allowed to discuss the topic and ask questions.

Tactile/Kinaesthetic Learners:

learn through moving, doing and touching...

A tactile/Kinaesthetic learner is someone who learns best by 'doing'. They learn best by physically experiencing the world around them. They excel at hands-on activities and will appreciate teachers who provide demonstrations which the kinaesthetic learner can duplicate.

Almost every child can be described as *predominantly* one of these types of learner. That does not mean that they can only learn in one way. They are usually a mixture of all three. However, they usually have a preference or a leaning towards one of the three in particular. As a parent it is up to you to make sure that they get the most out of their learning, by working towards the strengths of their particular learning style(s).

There are numerous free tests available online to help people find their particular learning style, but here is a method to quickly determine your own. Imagine that you are about to call a good friend on the telephone (without using the phone's memory). How do you remember the number?

If you remember seeing the number, or you have to look at the keys to dial, you are probably a visual learner.

If you have to say the number out loud or in your head as you dial, you are probably an aural learner.

If you do not even have to look at the phone to dial because your thumb 'knows' what to do, then you are probably a kinaesthetic learner.

There are a lot of assumptions made when teaching at primary school level which works in the children's favour.

- One of those assumptions is that the children do not all learn in the same way.
- Another is that in order to learn effectively, a primary school child cannot be expected to sit still all day listening to a teacher.

Either way, the end result is the same – primary schools make sure that during the average school day there is plenty of variety. Consequently, teachers will spend time talking to their students to *explain* their work (auditory). They will make sure that they spend time *showing* the students what to do (visual), and students also have the time to try and do the work themselves with (and without) the teachers assistance (tactile / kinaesthetic).

The reason that such a great deal of effort is put into providing an equality of learning opportunities is because the price of getting it wrong is very high. Whereas a teenager who is finding it difficult to access the curriculum will often switch off, go to sleep, find something else to do or even truant a lesson, the options for a primary school child are limited. Consequently, a primary school child that is having difficulty learning may cry, shout or scream, throw a tantrum or be destructive. Also, at that age, bad behaviour is very infectious. So it is in the teacher's best interest to keep their young children happy for as long as possible, as often as possible. This means catering to **everyone's** needs.

However, the reality of end of school exams and post-16 exams cannot be ignored. Regardless of any young persons learning style, they must learn to become adaptable enough to be able to be able to perform well in official examination conditions.

Summary

Why They Succeed In Primary: Recognition and Teaching to Different Learning Styles
<ul><li>Visual Learners learn through seeing, Auditory Learners learn through listening, Tactile/Kinaesthetic Learners learn through, moving, doing and touching.</li><li>Variety is extremely important in primary schools so that the students are constantly engaged, and do not get frustrated.</li><li>While the teachers make sure they offer a <u>varied</u> curriculum, they also help those students of <u>all</u> learning styles to succeed (whether accidentally or intentionally).</li></ul>

Learning By Synthesis & Creativity

As human beings, we are often accused of only using 10% of our brain's functions. "Could do better" on a child's school report itself is a pretty obvious statement of fact. We ALL could do a lot better!

One of the good things about primary school is that you have one teacher who is expected to teach you everything each year. The reason that is such a positive aspect of learning is that at any given time, the teacher can relate an aspect of a child's learning to any other aspect in the world. Links can be made in the classroom to bring clarity to abstract concepts and reinforce understanding. This is synthesis: The collection of little pieces of seemingly separate and distinct information to create a big picture and gain a wide understanding of a larger whole – holistic education. Within reason, a primary teacher can spend as long as they feel is appropriate to ensure that these links are fully explored.

Synthesising information in order to learn is a very African process.

This appears to be a hugely general statement. Hopefully, the following example will demonstrate the difference between a traditionally European and a traditionally African approach to learning.

31

To answer the question, "Is the universe growing?" a European scientist may study a small portion of our star system (analysis: break the whole into small pieces for study – the opposite of synthesis). After this study over a period of time, the scientist could make the assumption that these results would also occur on a much larger scale i.e. the universe.

A traditionally African approach could be (for example) to observe the spiral pattern of hair growth in the back of a human head and recognise that it is mathematically proportional to the spiral shape of a nautilus shell as well as the spiral shape of our galaxy. Using these examples of growth in nature on a small scale, it would be reasonable to not only assume that the universe is growing, but that perhaps the universe itself is a living organism!

I am not trying to assign a right or wrong way of coming to a conclusion, only that as people of African descent, we also have a *cultural learning style* of synthesising.

Ever noticed that children are wrong a lot more often in secondary school than they are in primary school. Is it because there are less right answers available the older you get? Surely the older and wiser we get, the more we should realise that there are a lot of ways to skin a cat. The truth is that in primary schools the ethos is such that teachers are simply a lot more open minded to the possibility that children may see truths that we as adults may not under-stand.

There is a heart-warming story that is told amongst the teachers at a particular Lewisham school. A student came in one morning with a beaming smile and proudly told his teacher,

"God took my picture last night!"

Coming from an adult, that statement would have many people searching for a number for social services. However, keeping in mind the child's innocent demeanour it was not long before the teachers realised that the almighty cam-era flash he saw was lightning! It just took a shift in perspective to understand.

The point being made is that we must be aware of one of the most obvious and important characteristics of our children – they speak their minds. It may be during the vows of a wedding when we hear, "I want to go wee, wee!" It might be on a crowded train when a child points to a stranger and says, "He smells funny!" Or it may be in a classroom to say, "I think the answer is seven!" However, we must also recognise that their eagerness to answer questions and speak their minds is directly related to the *manner* in which their comments are received.

In a primary school setting, children's responses are usually received with love, support and understanding. Even when those teachers hear an answer which they think is completely wrong, the child is still more likely to feel comforted by a teacher's response of, "Ooooh that was close", "Not quite" or "That's a good answer. Has anyone else got an answer?" Most importantly, a primary school teacher is more likely to take a step back and consider if there is another way of looking at the situation in order to understand their student's perspective. This is because most primary school teachers know the importance of creating an environment where their students feel safe to respond to questions openly and honestly. This is a great for creative students, lateral thinkers and those students whose willingness to speak in class is related to the backlash of shame or ridicule they are likely to receive if their comments are in error.

However, in secondary school, teachers are less nurturing of our children and seem less willing to accommodate different answers. Perhaps this is because of their long-term objectives of creating students who will be successful in examinations where there **are** only one or two correct possible responses. The narrowing of education into subjects at secondary school seems to also narrow the students' chances of giving correct answers! Is it any wonder that by Year 11 students are often scared stiff to present their ideas in front of the rest of their class, and we wonder where their enthusiasm for learning has gone!

Summary

Why They Succeed In Primary: Synthesis & Creativity
• Teachers have time and space to constantly make links with other parts of the whole curriculum. • Traditionally African method of communication (synthesising) is supported in Primary school level • Primary school allows children space to be creative with their answers and still be correct, so they are confident giving answers.

Part 3

Why They Fail In Secondary

Warning!

Turn to next chapter if you're used to blaming others for your responsibilities.

One of the main reasons for me writing this book is because many parents cannot figure out why there is such a drastic change in their children's achievement after leaving primary school. But at the same time, seem completely unaware of their own drastic changes in behaviour once their child entered secondary school.

Tony Warner of **Black History Walks** is an active educator of students, teachers, parents and elders across the country. When lecturing on the topic of education Tony begins with the assumption that as a bare minimum, parents can already answer positively to ALL of the following:

- You attend Parent Teacher Association (PTA) meetings or
- You are a school governor
- You have read the school policies and procedures
- Your child is enrolled with a Saturday School or mentoring group
- You are familiar with the National Curriculum
- You are already saving for University / Higher Education / Vocational fees
- You have read and digested **Tell It Like It Is**: *How our schools fail Black Children* edited by Brian Richardson

36

If you can answer positively to 6 out of these 7 points, you are not supposed to feel good about yourself! This is the bare minimum. If you were asked if you bathed once a day, do not expect a pat on the back and a handshake from the Mayor because you bathe once daily. That is the least you should be doing. It informs most people that you still either go to work, or get under your bed-sheets at night with a not-so-sweet bodily odour!

For reasons beyond reason, just because a child is attending secondary school and can cook themselves a meal, parents seem to think that is the end of the majority of their responsibilities as a parent.

Absolutely not!

This is the start of the most critical period of their lives. A period where:
- they begin to make decisions about the man or woman they want to be;
- they begin to adopt their own values and ethics;
- their choice of friends moves beyond simply the people in their class;
- they begin to look at long-term career options; and ultimately
- they begin to look at their purpose in life.

Naturally, these monumental life choices come with countless questions. Questions on:

- Racism;
- Insecurities and fears;
- Prejudice;
- Puberty;
- Attraction to opposite sex;
- Education;
- Work;
- Positive and negative peer pressure;
- Drugs;
- Carrying offensive weapons in 'self-defence';
- And even having children of their own!

The answers to these questions will play a huge part in helping these young individuals decide what and who they want to be.

It is important that they receive guidance from their parents on all matters concerning their future. Furthermore, it is of vital importance that the child looks to their parents as their <u>first</u> port of call when seeking advice on these matters for one basic reason,

There is nobody else on earth who will provide guidance with more love in their hearts for that child than their parents.

With that firmly in mind, it should be the fundamental duty of every parent from the moment of their child's birth, to continually work at ensuring their child is comfortable talking to them – about anything! At least then, when your 13 year-old daughter wants to know what to do when they like a boy, they don't get advice from 'Tracey' the well developed, been drinking since age 9, smoking since age 10 and sexually active with Year 11 boys since age 12, girl that sits next to your daughter in Religious Education!

Open lines of communication are especially important for fathers, who often think that their role is simply to correct 'bad' behaviour. There is nothing more comforting to a child than knowing that your father is in your corner at an emotionally stressful time. This is not because men are better at providing emotional support. Not by a long shot! Women have taken care of that job with distinction for thousands of years. The reason is because unfortunately, in times of a child's emotional stress, when a father makes their contribution, nine times out of ten, they end up *adding* to that stress. Therefore, a father in your child's corner during hard times should be recognised as a huge blessing.

Almost as important as communication with your child is the communication with the school. It is the easiest way to be kept informed and it will stop you making embarrassing statements which highlight your lack of awareness of significant events in your child's school life.

Statements such as:

38

I didn't know that <enter your child's name here>

...has changed tutor groups!
...has been entered for the lower tier paper!
...was moved out of the top set for behaviour reasons!
...has more than one teacher for English!
...was being taught by a trainee teacher / NQT! (Newly Qualified Teacher)
...has been truanting lessons!
...was excluded from lessons internally!

You would know all of this if keeping in contact with your child's teachers was a priority.

Here are some other baffling sentences often spoken at Parents Evenings and what the teacher *actually* hears.

Parents say...	Teacher hears...
I don't know why they said they didn't have enough time to finish the course-work, **they don't even have any chores to do!**	You have raised an irresponsible child. You are weak parents. Your child has probably got you both wrapped around their little finger.
I didn't know that their homeworks were not being completed!	The child comes home from school and does what they want without being challenged or monitored by parents.
I thought you liked English!	These parents probably have not spoken to their child about what subjects they enjoy in years.
...and what do you teach?	I am completely unconcerned with my child's academic progress, because we should already know who you are, what you teach, how well you teach and if our child enjoys your lessons.

However, the most classic line heard at parents evenings (which is only spoken by parents of <u>secondary</u> school children) is:

"But they told me they didn't have any homework!"

At this point, formal charges of 'parental incompetence' should be made.

Firstly, regardless of whether a child has been **given** homework, they should be doing school-related work between set times every day. Secondly, for some reason parents of secondary school children feel that their child should be responsible for all communication with the school rather than themselves. This is the laziest form of parenting. Why would a parent ask their child what was said by their teacher? There is absolutely no need for a 3rd person to be involved in that conversation. Your child is not required to be a translator or mediator between parent and teacher so simply remove them from the equation.

Do not give your child the huge responsibility of managing their future. That is the job of the <u>parent</u>.

Of course, completely bypassing your child in your communication with the school is not an unbreakable law. Feel free to keep them in the loop, but do not be dependent on them for important information. You should already have the email addresses for all of your child's teachers. If you want to know what grade they received for their last homework, ask them yourself!

Summary

Why They Fail In Secondary: Decreasing Parental Involvement
• Drastically reduced number of visits to school. Some parents think once a year for parents evening is satisfactory parenting!   • Have not read school policies, procedures or National Curriculum   • Child does not receive supplementary education or mentoring.   • Parents have allowed their child to stop talking with them.   • Parents make their child responsible for monitoring classwork and homework.

In English state secondary schools, the ethos is often the polar opposite of schools in Africa and the Caribbean. Teachers who have come from the Caribbean and especially West Africa utter the same 5 words in a state of total confusion when they try and teach children in this country,

"They don't want to learn!"

Experienced teachers in English schools shake their heads at the childish innocence of these overseas teachers. The unfortunate truth is that especially in inner-city schools, new teachers have to prove they can master the 'gladiator circle' (classroom) before the students will allow them the *privilege* of teaching them. Teachers from the African continent or the Caribbean know that most schools still employ corporal punishment. Additionally, most parents have to pay for their child's education. Either way, the consequences for a child refusing to study would be severe and immediate.

However in this country, the primary objective for the majority of students when walking into a class is to be entertained. So let's be completely honest. Messing with a weak teacher and watching them get flustered is very entertaining when the consequences are relatively insignificant. When we understand this basic objective, it is a lot easier to understand why the two most popular types of student in class are the ones who provide that entertainment:

1.   the class clown; and
2.   the insolent child.

The clown is obviously a favourite because they keep everyone laughing and stop lessons from becoming boring. They receive the most support from the students who find the work difficult, as they take the attention away from their own feelings of inadequacy in that subject.

The insolent child is feared, admired and (to a degree) respected because of their willingness to openly defy their teacher's instructions. They receive support from most students for the same reason that most people watch reality shows. It is entertaining to watch somebody (the teacher) fail and/or be humiliated.

Although the class clown can sit anywhere in the class and still be effective at low-level disruption, the insolent child is happiest at the back of the class. At the back, the fact that they are doing very little work can be ignored and they can cause the most disruption without the teacher (who is usually at the front of the class) being able to confidently identify which child is interfering with the learning of others.

With this class setup, negative peer pressure is a lot easier to understand. Disrupting the class is the popular choice, therefore getting on with your work and being a high-achiever often makes students unpopular. Many students who wish to get on with their work cannot even vocalise their frustration from the fear of going against the most feared individuals in the class as well as the other secretly less-able students who would prefer that the lesson did not continue.

These students who secretly long to get on with their work and achieve often prefer that their peers did not know their secret agenda. Unfortunately, there are a number of giveaways:

1.   Those who get good grades;
2.   Those who are respectful to their teachers;
3.   Those who sit at the front of the class;

4.   Those who stay behind after school voluntarily;
5.   Those who answer questions correctly; in fact
6.   Those who act like they care at all about their education.

Consequently, many students spend a great deal of effort trying not to let any-one know that they wish to achieve, and they perfect their acting skills so as to appear nonchalant about their academic progress. Have you ever seen a child win an award at primary school? Do you remember how proud and happy they were? What about a child that wins an award at secondary school? Did they give the impression of being proud? Or did they look irritated that they had to stand up, walk a few paces and collect a prize they didn't really want.

To manage both the expectations of their parents **and** their peers, some students even create an entirely new personality which they use in school. That individual is completely different from the child that arrives home from school in the afternoon and is courteous and respectful to their parents and their elders.

Teachers do not feel the need to inform parents of this behaviour because in secondary school, that behaviour is the 'norm'. Children do not wish to come home and explain in detail what happens in class in the fear that their parents will blow their cover. So begins the steady decrease in communication with their parents.

Naturally, many parents are left very confused about the apparently rapid change in their child's attitude towards school, and find themselves literally 'at war' with their child's friends whom they are constantly reminded "**all** act like that".

Parents of the 'multiple personality' children are often shocked at Parents Evening at the stories of this imposter mistaken for their child. They go home either in a state of denial or completely at a loss as to how to save their child's educational goals. Both responses are as detrimental to the child as each other. Denial does not help because if parents believe that every teacher is lying about their child, every subsequent call from school will be met with suspicion and hostility. The result is that contact from the school reduces and the child's behaviour worsens because of the decay of the home-school relationship.

Equally, giving up on your child has the exact same overall result. Clearly, the only positive action is to maintain regular contact with the school.

Realistically though, any parent who feels that speaking to their child's teachers only <u>once</u> in a year (at a Parent's Evening) cannot carry the title of 'parent'. Busy or not, that pathetic level of input into your child's education is inexcusable.

Parents, you must realise that this is the time to be brutally honest about your child's experiences in school. Telling your child not to submit to negative peer pressure in school is about as useful as saying "be careful" on the subject of teenage pregnancy. The intentions maybe good but without realistic, practical guidance, those good intentions will fall flat on their face.

Do not be naïve. It is almost impossible to give good advice to your child on a subject you know very little about, especially if the little you knew (back in the day) does not apply to your child now.

"Just be quiet and stay focused on your work"

Let's be honest, that is very difficult for most children if there are some good jokes flying around the class. For girls, jokes about other girls' dress sense or personal hygiene are especially hard to ignore. For boys, cusses about other boys' mums are especially hard to ignore. If you heard one student say to another,

"Your mum is so old, she was a waitress at the last supper!"

Do you honestly think your child will remember the information presented on the worksheet during that lesson, or that joke? Especially if the teacher is caught trying to hold back a chuckle, that just adds weight to the joke. Students will say, "Look, even the teacher's laughing at your mum!"

Rather than just tell your child to just ignore the class-clowns and insolent pupils and focus on the work (which you **should** do), put pressure on the school to provide training for teachers with poor classroom management skills. That way, you can be more confident that whilst your child is in a classroom, they are learning.

Rather than be surprised at parent's evening at academic and behaviour issues that you knew nothing about, maintain regular contact with your child's teachers. That way you are regularly informed and can constantly make adjustments to ensure the academic success of your child in school.

Negative peer pressure is one of the most significant factors to your child's educational demise in secondary school. Preparations must be made for its impact and it must be managed and minimised the moment your child steps foot in their new school otherwise its effects will grow, while the interaction with your child will steadily decrease.

Summary

Why They Fail In Secondary: Negative Peer Pressure
• Ethos in British schools is that students will try to stop teachers from teaching. A 'good' teacher is one that can *force* the children to learn! • Rude children and class clowns are often the most popular students. • Students do not want to be seen as weak, and so act as if they do not care about their grades to increase their popularity.

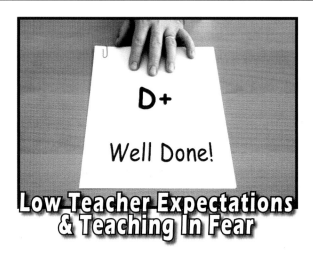

By the third year of secondary school (Year 9) the 'cute factor' is well and truly gone. The language used in primary school which helped the children to reach for the stars such as, "You can be *anything* you want to be" is replaced in secondary school with the more cynical, "If you don't get the grades, you won't be able to…" literally slamming shut doors of opportunity in every direction they turn. There is still room to use motivating language with our students whilst still being realistic. For example,

- "Without the higher grades you will have to put a lot more effort into your networking skills." or,
- "You can still achieve your goals, if you are prepared to…"

Teachers no longer identify students of African descent with their mental images of cute little babies who have the limitless potential to be anything they want to be. To many of their teachers, they now more closely resemble the stereotyped mental images they have of Black youth.

Males = violent, aggressive, academically slow, overly image conscious
Females = attitude, verbally aggressive, overly sexual, overly image conscious

These characteristics are clearly not the ones we would associate with motivated, independent learners. These are more like the characteristics of bottom-set or remedial learners, and subconsciously these are the unspoken targets that are set for our young learners. Their bad days are seen as the expected behaviour, quickly mentioned in the staff room by other teachers. Whereas the majority of the time when they are actively learning will later be commented on as surprisingly good behaviour (i.e. not what was expected).

Whilst listening to their child's account of the events of the day at school, parents must actively listen for those tell-tale indicators that all is not well in class. For example, the teacher seems to be shouting regularly, or the teacher feels the need to correct inappropriate behaviour in a degrading fashion rather than with love and respect. Those readers familiar with the book *The Celestine Prophecy* may recall the imagery of conversations as an interaction of energies. Arguments however, were described more as one person stealing the other's energy. When teachers are intimidated by students, one method often used to deal with that fear is to belittle those students. In this way it is easier to see that humiliation and over-reaction to challenging behaviour (with exclusions) is a means to recover from a sense of powerlessness, or a way to reclaim their lost energy (power).

Educational and social trends seem to be following many of the past US trends with respect to our youth. The increase in violence in our schools is reflection of the increase of violence on our streets. Additionally (as in the US), the government has had a profound impact on Black families by telling them that they cannot discipline their children which has had a knock-on effect in our schools. This result was best explained by Dr. Julia Hare at a 2007 conference, *'The State of Black America'*. Dr. Hare said[*], "When they made our parents afraid to discipline their children, what happened? We found out that:

> The classroom teachers are scared of the Head teacher,
> The Head teachers are scared of the Directors of Education,
> The Directors of Education are scared of the board of governors,
> The board of governors are scared of the parents,
> The parents are scared of the children,
> And the children ain't scared of anybody!"

---

[*] This has been paraphrased to relate to the British education system

In PTA meetings, parents should identify teachers who not only have low expectations of our children, but also have low expectations of *themselves*. For some of these teachers, they regularly work in fear of being ridiculed, verbally abused or even assaulted! They consider a day successful if they didn't have to call an assistant head-teacher to remove a student for them. What happens to the parent's expectations of academically stretching their child, when the teacher is just happy that he or she survived their worst teaching day of the week without anything in their classroom getting damaged. Teachers who are literally scared to be around our children cannot be expected to confidently demand better from those same students when they are underachieving.

These low expectations are more apparent the more students of African descent are in the class. The pace of the class moves even more slowly and the level of work set does not increase in line with their development until one day the teacher revisits their predicted levels / grades and realises that according to previous testing, their group is a lot more capable than they gave them credit for. At that point, most teachers dismiss the Key Stage 3 and Key Stage 4 predictions as not appropriate to students who attend their particular type of school.

The language used with many of our African & Caribbean students is also skewed. Teachers talk of the improved focus and effort that is required to achieve a "grade C". When talking to students of other backgrounds, the improved focus and effort are the requirements for an "A to C" grade. At what point were A and B grades not viable options to our children?

It seems that these expectations are also played out when decisions are made (often in private) concerning the tier of entry for our students sitting GCSE examinations. For some reason our children seem to be the subject of a worrying trend of being entered for lower-tier examinations for their own safety! Parents of African & Caribbean children are often told that it is safer for their child to be entered for a lower-tier paper than a higher-tier one in case they fall off the bottom of the scale and receive no level or grade at all. Be careful of this 'helpful' advice. Any teacher will can tell you that it is harder to get a level 5 on a 3-5 SAT paper than it is to get a level 5 on a 4-6 or 5-7 paper. Similarly, it is harder (not easier as some would lead you to believe) to achieve a grade C on a lower-tier exam (C – G) than it is to achieve a level C on a higher-tier exam (A* – D).

Readers of this book who are teachers in inner-city schools will have to bear me witness to these comments, or at least look again at classrooms with fresh eyes and ears to see if my comments are justified.

Whilst I have the attention of the teachers, let me draw your attention to something which probably affects the male African & Caribbean staff as much as it affects our African & Caribbean boys. You may have noticed:

- when intruders find their way onto your school site,
- when a potentially violent student must be removed from class, or even
- when a room needs to be cleared of all students quickly,

teachers and support staff of <u>African</u> descent are regularly called upon to act as some kind of in-house security team! Similarly, large African & Caribbean boys are often called upon by other teachers to act as a peace-keeping presence to other students. This has got to stop! If students are to take on extra responsibilities let it be officially as a prefect so that it can be noted on his CV. Let that role consist of **all** the responsibilities that come with that position, such as presenting assemblies to his peer groups, guiding parents viewing the school, contributing to the school newsletter/magazine etc. not just security and crowd control.

We must recognise the leaders in our young men and women and give them leadership responsibilities that demonstrate the type of expectations we have of them as future leaders of our community.

Summary

Why They Fail In Secondary: Low Teacher Expectations & 'Teaching In Fear'

- Teachers see Black children as the negative stereotyped images portrayed in the media. This results in lower expectations.
- Teachers with low expectations of themselves – just hoping to survive the day unscathed, instead of securing the academic future of their students.
- Teachers enter our children for lower-tier papers where the higher grades are impossible to achieve.
- Black children are given security guard responsibilities instead of 'real' roles of responsibility around school.

Behaviour Management & Consequences

Where does the nurturing of children's emotional growth become behaviour management? And where does correcting unsociable behaviour stop being guided by values of right and wrong but instead, replaced with threats of incarceration (detention) and withdrawal of education (exclusion)? Why, in secondary school of course!

Time-wasting is of the essence in a secondary school. Not enough time is dedicated to instilling moral values in the children. Instead too much time is spent chasing after mirages of academic excellence (e.g. 11+ and SAT examinations) to keep the students and teachers occupied. Not enough time is spent showing our children their proper roles in families, their roles and responsibilities in their communities, and ultimately their role and purpose in life. Consequently too much time is spent trying to give these children bright and sparkly goals to keep them occupied (e.g. new mobile phones, PSPs, plasma televisions, cars etc.).

No time at all is spent teaching our children how to commune with themselves and interact with others. The result is that our students are not physically, emotionally or spiritually prepared to make the most of a learning environment. The result of this lack of preparation is too much time is spent in classrooms trying to force behaviour patterns on the students keeping them quiet and still so at least they can act like good learners. Consequently, when they fail we issue

51

more and more punishments to our students as consequences for their failure to conform.

For some reason we have led ourselves to believe that nurturing is only useful whilst our children are small. Nurturing apparently is inappropriate once you grow past 4 feet in height. However, a wife expects to be nurtured by her husband in marriage and vice-versa. Both expect the other to meet their physical, emotional and spiritual needs. Both expect their wants in their relationship to be respected even if they cannot <u>all</u> be met. Both hope that they will be valued as a human being and treated accordingly. These are fair and realistic expectations for a relationship. But nurturing of the individual is all but abandoned in secondary school. Appropriate for infancy, appropriate for adulthood, but inappropriate for adolescence?

Let us look at some recent trends.

1. Corporal punishment has been removed from school[*].
2. The practice of any religion has been systematically removed from schools (at its most basic level 'religion' is a system of rules and procedures to govern your behaviour). Religion can now only be studied as a thing, rather than experienced by children as a lifestyle or part of their daily culture.
3. Authority in the classroom has been systematically removed from teachers.

But most interestingly, classroom management is **not** taught as a module on teacher training courses. Let me repeat that so that the statement has its proper impact.

Classroom management is **not** taught on teacher training courses.

It does not matter how much a teacher knows, he or she will be unable to impart any knowledge to a class if they are not able to get their students to listen.

---

[*] The author is not making a case to reinstate corporal punishment, he is only showing the trend of increasing freedom for children to behave in a manner which is ill-suited for learning.

Secondary schools have many questions to be answered. Perhaps one of the most important is why are they not designed to empower our students with knowledge rather than empowering the students with the authority to opt out?

Summary

Why They Fail In Secondary: Behaviour Management & Consequences
• **Practicing** excellent morals and ethics is not given priority status in school.
• Children are not taught how to interact with each other, so emotionally and socially immature people frequently get into trouble.
• Teachers stop nurturing the children (as if they are too old to be loved and respected!)
• Teachers are not taught how to manage classroom behaviour on teacher-training courses.

Awareness, But Rejection Of Teaching To Different Learning Styles

Secondary school teachers are well aware of the different learning styles. They are well aware that students with differing learning styles need to be stimulated in different ways. Although secondary school teachers may not be aware of how to plan lessons that cater to the 3 main learning styles*: visual; auditory and kinaesthetic, they are aware that a range of planning is required.

Remember:

Visual Learners: learn through seeing...

Auditory Learners: learn through listening...

Tactile/Kinaesthetic Learners: learn through moving, doing and touching...

Teachers should already be preparing lessons for different abilities in their classrooms. Preparation for 'differentiated learning' requires work for the less-able, work for the 'average' students and work for the high achieving students. That can mean 3 different sets of work for each lesson. So, if a teacher has an average of 4 lessons each day realistically, they could actually be preparing 12 different sets of work. There are 3 major learning styles: visual, auditory and kinaesthetic. Teachers that wish to deliver lessons accessible to these three different learning styles would have to do so for each of their ability groups, and

---

*   3 is the absolute minimum, some tests for learning styles can categorise the learner in up to as many as nine or ten different learning styles!

then for each of their lessons. That means that the preparation for 12 different sets of work would now have to be 36 different sets of work, just for one day! The majority of teachers do not plan their lessons for the different learning styles for one simple reason – it's too much work!

If you are an **auditory** listener then you are in luck because the majority of teachers stand at the front of the class for over half the lesson and just TALK. The vast majority of the rest of the teachers talk and use notes to support their lesson.

Teachers using standard whiteboards and/or interactive boards often use colour. This means that in some lessons the **visual** learner will be catered for (slightly!). However, most teachers give their notes to students by dictation or photocopied notes on white paper, which is not too stimulating for the visual learner.

Kinaesthetic learners spend most of their days tortured at school as they are usually forced to stay rooted to their chairs all day except for sports, dance or drama – where they naturally excel. Unfortunately, they are constantly reminded that they should not be so lazy in the 'more important' subjects such as English, mathematics, science and ICT.

As parents, it is our duty not only to identify what type of learner our child is, but also to tailor their study habits to suit their individual learning styles. A common negative occurrence that many parents experience is raising an academically successful child, then having a second child and repeating their 'successful' formula but having very different results. Sometimes, the second child even grows to dislike school not only because they are unsuccessful, but because they constantly hear their parents confusion and disappointment over why their methods are not working with *them*. Possibly, because the children concerned have different learning styles!

Summary

Why They Fail In Secondary: Awareness, but Rejection of Teaching to Different Learning Styles
• Parents do not support teachers by informing them of their child's learning style. • Teachers do not research or prepare lessons to engage all learners because of their difficult workload.

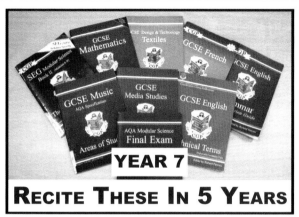

YEAR 7

RECITE THESE IN 5 YEARS

Learning By Analysis & Regurgitation

For the child of African descent, the change in the method of teaching is a drastic one. Traditionally, holistic learning is the style children have become amiliar with at primary school. Looking at the things around us in our immediate environment to provide an understanding of the 'big picture'. This is synthesis in action. However, on arrival to secondary school the technique is all but abandoned, replaced instead with rote learning, analysis and mindless regurgitation. It does not take an expert in psychology to predict the effects of following actions:

Action	Emotional Response
A high level of success in the majority of their primary school subjects	Happy, confident, enthusiastic
Move from primary to secondary school	Nervous, excited
Subjects not taught in a familiar way (analysis instead of synthesis)	Uncertain
Drop in level of success in previously comfortable subjects	Disappointment, confusion, resentment

Although most people prefer the security of what is known, it is not surprising that in Year 7 and 8 many African & Caribbean students are still reminiscing about the 'good old days'. It is not uncommon for these students to repeatedly comment on the fact that their primary school teachers were a lot better at their job than their secondary school counterparts.

The surprising thing is that the majority of secondary school teachers do not have the faintest idea what goes on in the average primary school. They remain blissfully unaware of the successful teaching methods used with their same students up until year 6. Nevertheless, they immediately shock their new intake with a brand new method of teaching to which they expect the students to immediately adapt, with little or no acknowledgement of their individual learning styles.

Students of African descent are some of the hardest hit as a result of this change. As mentioned earlier, this is because culturally, people of African descent generally communicate their ideas and solve problems in a holistic fashion. Naturally, in European schools the model for success is the model which best suits the European – analytical.

Even though many talk about holistic education sometimes it is not obvious what that actually looks like, especially if it has never been pointed out, so some examples are given below:

Topic	Analytical	Holistic
Mathematics: Percentages	Study different uses of percentages in isolation.	Find out the costs involved in raising a child.
English: Classic 'love stories'	Watch Romeo & Juliet, then identify how 'love' manifested itself in that story.	Find a long-standing couple in your family and find out the secret of their success.
Art: Explore the theme of "flight" in the major religions	Study the works of recognised artists to create their own piece.	Deliver an oral, visual and physical presentation on the importance of prayer.

The holistic activities may seem abstract in comparison to the tasks (or objectives) that have been set. What is important to note is that the analytical activities themselves were very prescriptive, very similar to those given at GCSE level in secondary school. The analytical activity is a typical method that may be used to achieve the objective(s) of the given topic. The holistic activity is one that is highly likely to achieve the objective *whilst* learning an important life-lesson. In a more holistic framework, the original topic instead of being as specific as "percentages" for example, may have simply been "financial planning".

In his book ***The United Independent Compensatory Code/System/Concept,*** Neely Fuller clearly states that the purpose of education is to find <u>truth</u>. Arguably, when studying the dynamics of relationships, it would not be a useful exercise to simply memorise the seven basic plots* used in literature, television and film:

1.   Overcoming The 'Monster';
2.   Comedy;
3.   Rags to Riches;
4.   Voyage & Return;
5.   The Quest;
6.   Rebirth; and
7.   Tragedy.

It may be a refreshing change to engage the synthesising part of the brain and talk to grandparents about their marriage. However, this may not help with examination questions which are very specific in how they test certain criteria.

The ideal solution would be a 'marriage' of the two. Considering the plummeting numbers of our young people choosing to get married, and the escalating numbers of divorces of those that do, there seems a desperate need of guidance on how to **stay** married. If we acknowledge that each of us have our own life-story, then the seven basic plots of a story should still apply.

---

*   From the book, The Seven Basic Plots: Why We Tell Stories by Christopher Booker.

1. **Overcoming The Monster** could be managing to overcome past personal issues of rejection for example. These issues could be jeopardising the relationship because each unintentional act of 'rejection' from one spouse is followed by an apparently huge over-reaction from the other spouse.

2. **Comedy** in a marriage is obviously sought after however, a couple sometimes have to look at how to manage their relationship when they have slightly different senses of humour.

3. Financial security is a must in a marriage. Unfortunately, finances are one of the major reasons for marriage splits. Here, an age-old saying must be followed. "If you fail to plan, then you are makings plans to fail." A couple must sit down regularly to plan their own **Rags to Riches** transformation.

4. **Voyage & Return** describes some form of journey where new experiences are brought back home to improve the marriage.

5. **The Quest** speaks of another timeless African proverb, "Love is not just looking at each other, but looking in the same direction together." Married couples must have a vision of where and who they want to be in years to come, and make concrete plans to ensure these goals are achieved.

6. Most of the time **Rebirth** in a marriage is not as dramatic as one spouse suddenly becoming a born-again Christian. However, there are times when one spouse has a life-changing experience which forces them to view their environment (and often the people in it) completely differently. Managing rebirth in a marriage is often very difficult, as any married individual who has experienced a mid-life crisis will tell you.

7. Knowing, or learning how to support your spouse in a time of **Tragedy** can often be a defining moment. It can irreparably tear marriages apart or cement them so that they become unbreakable.

At such a critical time when reclaiming the African family unit is a major priority, parents will have to decide the best method of learning (analytical or holistic) for their child. This will depend on their particular goals, passing exams or finding truths. Hopefully, parents will endeavour to find a way in which both can be satisfied at the same time.

Summary

Why They Fail In Secondary: Learning By Analysis & Regurgitation
<ul><li>Students are shocked at sudden change of teaching style.</li><li>Teachers are unaware of the success of previous learning techniques used in primary school.</li><li>Balance of holistic – analytical learning is lost in preference to completely analytical learning.</li></ul>

Part 4

Improvements

Parental Involvement

Parental involvement is like a pension or a will. We all know that the preparations must be done early so that we are not caught unawares, but like a lot of people, we put them off again and again and then are surprised when an unfortunate turn of events places us in desperate need of one. Unfortunately, at the exact moment you need it the most, it's too late. Everything that happens after that moment is simply 'damage control'.

Before your child enters secondary school, make sure that you have mastered the following points. Remember, communication is the biggest key to avoiding the 'Secondary Slump'. Everything must be done to ensure that you and your child keep talking and get comfortable confiding in each other.

- If necessary, gossip with your child – even if it is about other members of your family. Just make sure that your family are well aware of the information being exchanged.
- Your child must never see you over-react to a comment they made to you in confidence. Treat every secret as a practice-run for the next one which is guaranteed to be bigger.

- Your regular contact with school will already have you well informed of the usual (and unusual) events of the school week. Nevertheless, everything that happens in that school should be relayed to you by your child so you can make the necessary changes to improve their achievement as soon as possible. This has the added benefit of conditioning your child to have the expectation that there is an efficient and unbreakable chain of contact between school and home.

The continual academic improvement cycle has increased importance when your child moves into secondary school.

Preparation:
The assessment of the school, its teachers and procedures must be a lot more thorough than before. At secondary level the new school will have more students to manage and your child will have a lot more teachers. Unfortunately, that means it will be a lot easier for your child to fall through any cracks in their system. This assessment should be a termly routine as teaching sets change all the time.

Be especially vigilant of your child's teaching sets. For example, they may be in teaching set two for both English and Mathematics (set one being the top set), which initially may not sound problematic. However, if there are five teaching sets altogether for English but only two for Mathematics this means that effectively, they are in the bottom set for Mathematics. The number of these inconsistencies will depend on how the students were timetabled.

Daily Debriefing:
Each day, after returning from school, your child should inform the parents of the events of the day as well as discussing what was considered positive and negative. Together with the child, parents discuss how to maintain what went well and how to make improvements on the less successful elements of the day.

Do not let your child get away with one word responses! Make sure you extract as much detail as possible.

- If you child is a **visual** learner get them to reproduce the diagrams or charts they looked at.
- If your child is an **auditory** learner, get them to repeat what was said
- If your child is a **kinaesthetic** learner, get them to demonstrate what they learned.

If they still insist on responding with one word sentences, tell them that the other option is to write daily essays titled, "My Day At School". They will quickly choose the easier option of *telling* you about their day.

Monitoring:
Parents then set up methods of monitoring the effectiveness of the changes they have put in place. This could be achieved by informing the relevant teachers, monitoring test results, asking one of your child's classmates to support them etc.

Implement:
After the necessary changes have been made, their effectiveness is checked. The new conditions that have been created following the implementation of the new strategies are re-assessed so that the improvement process can start over again.

- Schedule a regular interrogation of your school staff regarding your child's progress. Parent's Evening is any evening you want it to be!
- If you don't like the fact that your child has 3 different teachers for a single subject, get a group of parents to complain. Trust me the school will make timetabling a priority for your children as soon as possible!
- Do not pay for private tuition unless your child is already seeing all of the teachers weekly for free personal tuition after school. The school must provide that service if requested – they are not doing you a favour.
- Become a governor at your child's school. Many battles have been fought to include culturally relevant material on the national curriculum. However, it is still up to the school which items are selected. Most parents are not even aware that there is a choice. As a governor you will have the position to positively influence the learning environment of hundreds of children (after all, its not just Black children who benefit from a wider curriculum!)

65

Choosing & Monitoring Your Child's Peers

Choose my child's peers? Choose my child's friends for them? Can I do that?

Yes of course you can! It's called being a responsible parent!

I often proudly tell my friends how when I was at primary school, my mother would only let certain friends of mine in the house. Even if a group of us arrived together, Ben and Jamie would have to wait outside on the pavement for the rest of us to come out. On the pavement! They were not even allowed to wait inside the front gate! And what cardinal sin did they commit to be banished from the house forever? The first (and only) time that they came to the house, they did not say hello to my mother when they entered (my mother was in the kitchen at the time), and they did not say goodbye when they left!

If you are scratching your head wondering what the problem was, it may be because your culture is more English than African. The rest of my friends took off their shoes as soon as they entered the house then quickly asked, "Where's your mum and dad?" When they were getting ready to leave, they made sure that they knocked on the kitchen door, opened it (without going in) and said goodbye. Even the well-mannered English friends who had never been to a 'coloured ' person's house before made sure they followed *my* lead.

After that, word spread around primary school very quickly about the expectations for any child who came to our house. Funnily enough, **every** child from then on managed to meet those expectations. That included my 'gypsy' friend who I played with when I lived in Shepherds Bush. Anthony took a bath on the evening before he came round, on a day that was **not** his 'bath night' .

As soon as your child is able to socialise with other children, you should be making the appropriate efforts to ensure that your child is not in the company of too many undesirables. Your parents will have referred to them with any number of identifiers: bad-breed pickney; fool-fool children; no-wherians etc.

Obviously, to do this effectively you need to be aware of all of your child's friends as well as some of their associates. Again, this places a strong emphasis on keeping the lines of communication open.

However, (and this may seem like a contradiction) a mobile phone should be out of the question. When mobile phones were initially being marketed to the public, it was as a tool for those adults who worked in the business sector. Once that market was saturated, they were marketed as a fun means of communication to college and university students, then students in general. The biggest growing market for mobile phone companies in 2008 are 8-9 year-olds. The marketing agenda now is 'safety'.

You can make sure that your child is safe by giving them a mobile phone which can be used to and from school.

Although there is truth to this statement, what is not acceptable is the fact that with a mobile phone, your child can create and maintain extremely intimate relationships completely without your knowledge. Secondary school teachers will testify that mobile phones in schools are used by students:

- to get their friends hooked-up with potential boyfriends/girlfriends;
- to coordinate fights in and out of school; or
- to call for back-up when trouble is brewing.

With movie capture software, it is not unusual for a large number of students in a school to know the identity of certain boys who have secretly used their phones to show other male friends what certain girls are 'up for'. This puts a lot of girls at serious risk.

Many say that with the technological developments of the age that we live in, it is natural that there will be side-effects using certain products. My argument is that for the exact same reason, we must be even more critical of the products we give to our children, simply because they saw an attractive poster or television commercial.

Not much more needs to be said on the obvious pitfalls of MSN and other internet chat-room services. Here, the potential for danger is heightened because often you cannot see or hear the individuals you are talking to. An increasing number of reports to child protection services are confirming that paedophiles have flocked to MSN for obvious reasons. Although unnecessary, if chat-rooms are to be used at all by your child, make sure it is under the most strict supervision. The easier option is to encourage your friends parents to purchase landline phones with 'conference call' capability so that you all know who your child is in contact with.

As well as avoiding harmful situations, you can be proactive and encourage positive interactions with new peers. One of the important factors in the development of a confident child is removing their fear of new environments. Therefore, it is important that you make the effort to take your child out of their comfort zone every now and then to experience something positive and new. Almost every primary school girl plays netball, and the boys play football. See if there is anywhere your child can do something different like canoeing, fencing, or horse riding. Something which will make them stand out of the crowd and be proud of their uniqueness. If they get used to it with a hobby then it's likely that they will not be so afraid to stand out of the crowd with excellent grades in school.

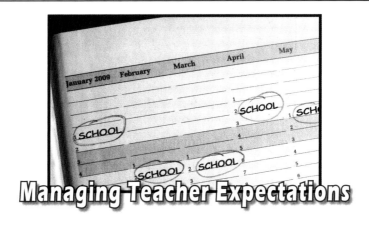

Managing Teacher Expectations

If your child is new to Year 7, then as far as the teacher is concerned, they are likely to be one of between 30 and 150 new students they will have to get to know. Unless your child is extremely disruptive, their teachers are unlikely to even know your child's first and last name by the end of September!

After the first term you will be considered lucky if even two of your child's teachers have any clue what your child is capable of with respect to their particular subject. After a couple of months they may vaguely remember what Key Stage 2 results your child achieved. But realistically, it's only by January that the teachers will start getting to grips with who they are dealing with as individuals. By then, who knows what bad habits your child has formed since joining the school.

The best form of introduction to a secondary school is one that immediately lets your child know that they have just stepped into the big leagues. They will be pushed harder than they have ever been pushed, and that the expectations are higher than they have previously experienced. However, your child *should* also feel that they will be supported by an experienced network of professionals in partnership with your parents to provide the best opportunities for success.

Due to the size of the building, the size of the student population and the size of the oldest students, most schools do not have to try very hard to give their new Year 7 students the impression that things have significantly changed.

However, weeks 5 and 6 are the all important markers to indicate the 'normal' working conditions of your child's secondary school. By week 5 your child should have received at least 3 marked home-works from each subject. This is about the time when most teachers not only start to fall behind with their marking and planning, but also fall back into their usual modes of working.

After 5-6 weeks of teaching and learning (do not include orientation period), this is when you need to give all of your child's teachers a wake up 'slap in the face' and call them to attention to *your* child's needs. Call a meeting with all of your child's teachers or request that every one of their teachers calls you at home to discuss progress, achievement and expectations. It is your job to make sure that each and every teacher knows what to **expect** and what to **accept** from your child.

A lot of parents do not think they have the authority to make such a request, or they don't want to inconvenience the teachers. Remember, teachers work for you.

- Find out when they have faculty, pastoral or full staff meetings at the school so that there are no clashes with your intended meetings.
- Say that you do not mind going to each of *their* classrooms. This is so the teachers are as comfortable and relaxed as possible when discussing your child to help the process of supporting your child cooperatively.
- Do not be the parent who gives every teacher a hard time just because you have unresolved issues from your childhood. It may be entertaining *once*, but your child will not benefit in the long-run.
- Unless there are serious issues, make your meetings quick because then the teacher will be happy to meet again if they found it a relatively painless exercise. Additionally, this will keep your child on their toes if they see that you have a positive relationship with their teachers.
- Make sure that your next meeting is scheduled in their diary for approximately 6 or 7 weeks later (i.e. next half term) to evaluate the success of all action points.

After this meeting, when you have left the school building if you have done a good job, the teachers will say to each other, "That parent's going to be trouble". Translated, that means, "That parent is going to make sure I do my job properly!"

Some parents feel as though secondary school is the time to give their children a little distance to mature into young adults.

Wrong!

If there is one thing that a young adolescent does not need any help with, it's creating distance between themselves and their parents. You might as well try to teach people from the Bahamas to take things easy and enjoy life. *They* won't need your help either!

At the time when these children have just started to define themselves, their ideas and their dreams, one of the most important factors in their development is the amount of nurturing and support they receive to 'be all they can be'.

Get to know your child's class tutor and let them get to know as many positive things that are happening with your child in <u>and</u> outside school. Do not assume they know everything that happens in school because they are their tutor. They have their own classes to teach and usually, are only informed of the negative incidents concerning children in their tutor group. Do not give them personal information that would be considered as 'family business'. This is mainly for two reasons:

1. Firstly, you do not really know these people or the stereotypes and prejudices they may have formed regardless of all the 'right' things they may say. You do not know how vindictive they may be with personal information Just keep it simple – they were top in the class in the last science test, they were chosen as vice-captain of the hockey team etc.

2. Secondly, you do not want to have the opposite effect that you intended by alienating yourself from your child because they felt that you betrayed their trust.

Fathers, a special warning to you. Do not become one of those parental figures who has nothing positive to say, then are shocked when your child says that they thought:

*   you hated them;
*   you just don't like children;
*   you wanted a child of the opposite sex;
*   you always considered them to be a disappointment.

That's what happens when you've got nothing positive to say!

Do you know what else happens? If you have a girl, you'll find out about her being sexually active the same day she's rushed to the hospital in labour. If you have a boy, you'll find out whether he listened to your advice on negative peer pressure when he asks you to say that he was with you all day on the 12th of last month should any police officers ask.

Dads of all kind must throw away this notion that being a strong father-figure translates only to being a domineering, miserable, one syllable speaking troll! Some fathers actually believe that 'always being there for their child' really means 'I will speak to my child every time they do something the wrong way, just to let them know what the right way is'. Seriously, keep a log book if you have to, but do whatever it takes to make sure that any criticism you have of your child is a rare occurrence. Tell your wife to remind you that you are not allowed to criticise your child unless you have praised them at least three times previously.

Do not think that this is a promotion of 'doormat parenting,' where discipline is all but abandoned in favour of bending to the **wants**, rather than the needs of your child. Absolutely not! Children need boundaries. In time they will recognise the importance of the discipline used in their own upringing.

Nonetheless, if you manage to convince your child that as parents, you are a safe port of call for any questions that they may have, and that their teachers at school have a genuine interest in their well-being, you will have gone a long way to secure an emotionally secure future for your child in school.

Maximising The Strengths & Minimising The Weaknesses Of Your Child's Particular Learning Style

Remember, in respect to learning styles, it is unlikely your child is only visual, only auditory or only kinaesthetic. They will most likely be a combination of all 3 with a preferred style within that range of learning styles.

From a teacher's perspective, it hurts when a student comes into class after a disappointing Parent's Evening with every intention of trying their best. However, because they are not equipped with the correct tools to help them learn they just cannot assimilate the information. Consequently, they become disenchanted and their efforts sink to an all-time low as they see their best efforts amount to nothing. Hopefully, the information presented in the next pages will allow parents to support their children regardless of their learning style.

New efforts according to a child's particular learning style means new equipment as well as a change of attitude from students and especially parents.

74

Aids for Visual Learners

Issue	Action
Visual learners need to see the teacher's body language and facial expressions to fully understand the content of a lesson.	It is better if they sit at the front of the classroom to avoid visual obstructions (e.g. people's heads).
They may think in pictures and learn best from visual displays including: diagrams, illustrated text books, overhead transparencies, videos, flipcharts and hand-outs.	Some exercise books have one side of lined paper followed by a side of plain. Use these as it will allow them to draw diagrams, flow-charts etc of their work whenever needed.
Visual learners learn words by analysing their component parts.	Try writing the words on paper, tearing them apart and putting them back together again. Make sure their dictionary is one that breaks the words into syllables as well as providing the definitions.
Visual learners are switched off by drab, plain surroundings.	Provide your child with coloured pens, markers, highlighters and paper so that they can colour-code their work. A small white board with coloured post-its would also be useful at home. Don't be afraid to offer teachers some posters to go up in their classrooms if they are too dull for your child's needs.

Aids for Auditory Learners

Issue	Action
Auditory students learn best through verbal lectures, discussions, talking things through and listening to what others have to say.	Watch out for the old-school, disciplinarian teacher who does not like any talking in their lesson. If they stand at the front of the class and talk a lot, then your child might be okay. However, If they just hand out textbooks and expect the child to get on with the work by themselves, and if they do not allow group work or paired work in their class, your child is going to have major difficulties. Get your child out of 'Shawshank' by any means necessary.
Auditory learners interpret the underlying meanings of speech through listening to tone of voice, pitch, speed and other nuances.	It is essential that your child sits around the quieter students. Definitely not gossips or the class clown. It will not matter where in the classroom they sit as long as the teacher can be clearly heard.
Written information may have little meaning until it is heard.	Auditory learners often benefit from reading text aloud which you can do with them at home. Additionally, they may benefit from using a digital voice recorder (with the school's permission) to help make notes after lessons. A good way of testing your child's understanding is to get them to explain their work to you. The best academic support you can give an auditory child is a study partner who is also an auditory learner so that they can discuss their work with each other.

Aids for Kinaesthetic Learners

Issue	Action
Kinaesthetic learners are accused of being disruptive often because in class they will wiggle, tap their feet or move their legs whilst in their seat.	To avoid being labelled ADD, request teachers find ways for kinaesthetic learners to physically answer questions or demonstrate their understanding through movement – even if it's answering problems at the board. Give your child a stress ball or other discrete physical activities they can do whilst in class.
Kinaesthetic learners need to move whilst they learn.	If they do not enjoy reading find plot-oriented books. They child often reflects action with body movement as they read. Kinaesthetic learners may need an exercise bike, treadmill or rowing machine in their later school years to help them study. Whereas other learners can study in chunks of 1 hour or more, kinaesthetic learners should work for 20-30minutes with 5-10 minute breaks.
Parents have low expectations for kinaesthetic learners believing they will only be happy doing manual labour.	Kinaesthetic learners (approximately 30% of population) make excellent engineers, artists, performers, actors, etc.

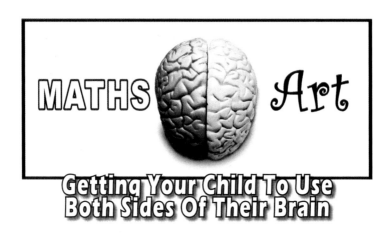

Ancient Egyptian Hieroglyphic language is the only language in history to actively use both hemispheres (sides) of the brain when reading and writing due to its pictorial script. It would seem that during the crusades to 'civilise' the continent of Africa, Neither Asia's or Europe's finest could duplicate this whole-brain mode of communication. Today, all languages engage only the left-side of the brain in their use.

This table basically explains the differences between left-brain and right-brain thinking:

Left Brain (Left Hemisphere)	Right Brain (Right Hemisphere)
Logical Sequential Rational Analytical Objective Looks at parts	Random Intuitive Holistic Synthesising Subjective Looks at wholes

To put it simply, primary schools take the time to engage in left and right brain activities. The result is simple – well-rounded successful individuals (on the whole). Secondary schools favour left-brain activities as 'higher thinking' activities. Left-brain approaches to subjects focus on rationally logical thinking, analysis and accuracy. On the other side, right-brain approaches focus on aesthetics, feeling and creativity.

As has previously been mentioned, one is not better or worse than the other. However, if traditional African principles of balance and reciprocity are followed, it would seem clear that the highest levels of thinking occur when both sides of the brain work harmoniously.

African scholars should be wary of leading people to believe that the African holistic form of education is the right way of learning in contrast to the rational form. That is <u>not</u> true. However, teaching in a holistic style is a good way to provide balance to an education system in this country which is almost entirely rational, but balance must be the main objective.

Teachers reading this book should concentrate on providing a whole-brain learning experience using metaphors, analogies, role-playing visuals and movement into their reading, calculation and analytical activities. However, if the teacher is only willing to stand at the front and lecture continuously, the responsibility falls on the parents to create right brain activities for your child's GCSE subjects. Remember, if the job is too great, call on other parents to work together for the benefit of your children. It takes the whole village to raise a child!

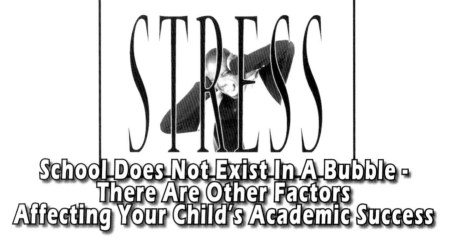

As tremendous as this book has been so far (it's okay, you can say it), it is not the answer to all your problems. There are numerous factors outside school which can affect the success of your child in secondary school. The following are just a few potentially significant factors which many teachers witness:

- Puberty
- Family drama
- First love
- Fear of academic failure
- Victim of bullying
- Confusion over career path
- Over-achieving older sister / brother
- Responsible for the welfare of younger siblings
- Death in the family
- Moving home
- Too many people living in the house

- Nowhere in the house to study
- Single parent working all hours
- No money for regular meals

- Low self esteem caused by:
  o Acne
  o Weight
  o Height
  o Race
  o Looks
  o Sexuality
  o Disability
  o Sexual abuse
  o Physical abuse
  o Abusive extended family member

- Alcohol issues in family
- Substance abuse issues in family
- Incarcerated family member or friend
- Gang pressures
- Pressure to lose virginity
- Pressure to disrespect teachers
- Pressure to not complete homework regularly
- Pressure to fight other students
- Trauma from refugee experiences

This list is only a reminder to parents to keep an open mind as you try to manage the many factors which can affect your child's academic progress. Keep in mind that it may not be *your* child! A change in your child's behaviour could also be because one of their friends is going through a really tough period, and they are struggling to support them.

Part 5

Solutions &
Models For
Success

There are only 4 real models for supporting your child's educational needs. As parents, you must identify what you (and your support network) are capable of providing. In order of quality, these models are:

1. African Holistic Education
2. Home-Schooling
3. Supplementary Education
4. Supported Education

African Holistic Education

To immediately clear up any confusion that may be felt with the chapter heading, African Holistic Education does not mean:

- A faith-based school
- The same as an independent or state school, but just with Black staff
- A regular school with the subject of African History taught regularly.

No, an African Holistic Education would comprise of many elements that in this society we would not be used to. Elements which are not only vital to the balanced growth and development of any human being, but which are especially important to the development of Africans in the Diaspora and on the continent itself. As a <u>minimum</u>, these would be:

1. Language (African)
2. African History (from Ancient Civilisations to present)
3. History of African Spirituality & Meditation
4. Agriculture
5. Literature
6. Nutrition & Health

7.   Political Science
8.   Economics, Finance & Budgeting
9.   Life Sciences: plumbing, electrical, carpentry & masonry
10.   Astrology & Numerology
11.   Interpersonal & Intrapersonal Skills Management
12.   Physical Education & Martial Arts Self-Defence

1.   <u>Language (African)</u>

You cannot create an African world-view in a student unless they can communicate and reason in a language that carries their **own** culture, traditions and values. That is like having a computer theory class without a computer. By simple logic, an African should not be trying to uplift themselves using the language of the people who enslaved you – a language which carries European culture, traditions and values. Culture, traditions and values that justified:

- the transatlantic slave trade,
- the genocide of the Native Americans,
- the genocide of the Native Australians,
- even the genocide of Europeans with minimal traces
  of African blood (Jews).

Those trained in arguing against uniting African people worldwide quickly point out,

"But Africa has so many languages!"

So does Europe! But most agree that the choices for learning a European language (other than English) are French, German, Spanish and Italian. The choice is not as impossible as many would have you believe. The most widely spoken is Swahili. Failing that, the choice should be the language of the country most likely to be visited e.g. Hausa (Nigeria), Twe (Ghana), Wolof (Senegal, Gambia), Zulu (South Africa, Zimbabwe) etc.

2.   African History (from Ancient Civilisations)

The history from the eyes of the conquerors must be reclaimed, rewritten and re-taught. An emphasis must be placed on the Ancient civilisations and how to recreate their former glory with the military presence to maintain it.

3.   History of African Spirituality

African spirituality must be de-mystified and Ma'at acknowledged as the first belief system which is still present in the major religions.

4.   Agriculture

African soil is still being stolen from the rightful owners. The land must be repatriated and re-cultivated primarily for the benefit of the Africans in Africa rather than the crops required by European nations.

5.   Literature

Every form of writing has been mastered by Africans on the continent and in the Diaspora. The fictional, non-fictional and political works of African writers must be given the position of benchmark to which all other literary works must aspire to.

6.   Health & Nutrition

One of the most carcinogenic items in our diet – processed sugar, and increasingly numerous cloned foods in our diet must be removed, followed by a hasty return to a natural balanced diet.

7.   Political Science

The same political manoeuvres have been used on different parts of the African continent, then in the Caribbean before the techniques are perfected in the slums, ghettoes and inner-cities across the world. These techniques must be studied in combination with master-texts such as **Yurugu** as a primary form of self-defense for Africa nations worldwide.

8.   Budgeting, Economics & Finance

Money management is of prime importance, firstly at an individual level, then at organisational level and finally on an international level, especially if a strategy to free African nations from the tyranny of the World Bank is to be implemented.

9.   Life Sciences: plumbing, electrical, carpentry & masonry

There is little point raising the necessary finances to purchase a house if it cannot be maintained. These are the bare essentials to support your family.

10.   Astrology & Numerology

This will have been touched on with the astronomy that would have been covered in the study of African Spirituality. It is one of the most ancient methods of understanding the world around us and the human connection to the heavenly bodies surrounding us.

11.   Interpersonal & Intrapersonal Skills Management

This is a direct move to create a more powerful society of leaders with Neuro-linguistic programming, networking and team-building skills.

12.   Physical Education With Martial Arts Self-Defence

This is the final element of the powerful unity of mind, spirit and body working positively in harmony. The self defence element, as well as being practical also provides the discipline to control the energy flowing through the body.

Home-Schooling

Your child has done reasonably well in their Key Stage 2 examinations. However, your local authority has said that you are out of the catchment area for the school that you wanted your child to go to. The only options they have left you with are schools with very bad reputations in terms of GCSE pass percentages and student behaviour. You would rather not send them at all, but you have no choice…right?

Especially when you have limited options in terms of the quality of local state schools, home-schooling should be a serious consideration and it is not as difficult as it sounds.

If one of the parents/guardians works freelance, does shift-work, or works on short contracts, home-schooling is an excellent option. If you know someone who is a teacher, they can borrow some books from school in the core subjects. These books usually cover the entire curriculum but many resources are also available online. A timetable can be quickly hammered out (like the one shown overleaf) which your child can carry with them at all times whether they are at grandma's house or their uncle's house or staying with a friend until you get back. You still talk through their day as if they were still at school. The continued dialogue is of the utmost importance.

If you know other parents in the same position, **pool your resources** and let your children study together. This will go at least some way to restoring the missing social aspect of school.

Obviously, one of the main benefits of home-schooling is the decrease in restrictions for daytime activities, courses and field-trips. Without the restrictions of the school day, a home-schooled child should be out of the house at least twice a week.

One trip should be to a local leisure centre which they should be able to use for free. That covers their P.E. lesson, but you should also look at the other activities they offer in the evenings such as martial arts, circuit training and yoga. They may also run courses such as typing (always useful!), computing, pottery etc. Keep in mind that you are trying to stimulate both sides of the brain and produce a well-rounded individual.

Their weekly field trip should be used as an opportunity to put their learning into perspective and make it **real**. Journeying around London is relatively cheap with a travel-card or oyster card. Travelling around the country by train is also relatively inexpensive as long as you can book at least a week in advance. Visit parks, art galleries, museums, films, shows, concerts. Stretch their boundaries. Let them meet people from across the country. Make sure that they recognise that there are African communities from Lands End to John O Groats. Conflicts over postcodes and areas can be treated as insignificant and petty by most 11 and 12 year-olds when they have seen more than just their estate, their school and the buildings in between.

Parents, you must explain the differences between:

- Where you live (resident);
- Where you have electoral rights (citizen); and
- Who you are (African, European, Asian etc.)

A great deal of work has been done on the African community to make them believe that they are not African. In fact, any other classification can be justified. It is only the label "African" which (in their mind) is unacceptable.

If on holiday in Italy a person saw a Chinese man and told a friend, I doubt that person would say that they saw:

1. A yellow man;
2. A Chino-Italian man; or
3. A person of colour.

They would probably just say they saw a Chinese man!

The fact that you happened to be in Italy, England, India or South America wouldn't change who he was. He might speak Italian, or even have Italian citizenship, but he would still be a Chinese man who happened to be in Italy. These discussions must be the starting point of the home-schooled Citizenship lessons.

On a smaller scale, parents must show their child the folly of fighting over land (Hackney, Peckham, Harlesden etc.) that they don't even own. Furthermore, owning land that **can** be passed down to your children is a realistic venture if they see the African continent as home rather than the UK.

Also, remember that home-schooling does not mean that your child will not be able to sit their SAT or GCSE examinations. You simply pay the cost of the exams to your local authority and they will let you know where the child can sit the papers at a registered centre.

Parents can be very intimidated about trying to teach a subject that they struggled with, or perhaps did not even study. However, as strange as it sounds, this shared anxiety can actually be a really good bonding experience for the both of you. When you put your child in the rare position of being the teacher, you might be surprised how they rise to the challenge of the added responsibility. Additionally, it will be a new experience for your child to be in a position where you need *their* help to understand the work. Let them enjoy it!

For those willing to go the extra mile, sit the GCSE exam with your child so that you completely share the experience of learning together. However, make sure it is not in the same school or exam centre. Remember, they love you but they may not want to be seen with you whilst around their peers.

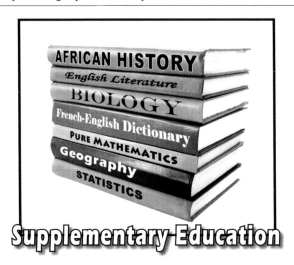

Without an African Holistic Education, or the option of home-schooling, you are forced to send your child into an independent school or a state school. As a parent, this is now a simple matter of 'damage control'. The question now is, how well you can deal with the psychological damage caused from full immersion in the British secondary education system?

One method of countering these negative effects is to give your child a supplementary education. Traditionally, these have been provided by Saturday schools or by churches at Sunday school. Many church regulars make sure that their child attends youth service or other positive activities that their church members can supervise. This has been a feature of African-centred schools since the days of Ancient Egypt where education was considered a sacred institution. Where all knowledge was considered a gift from the Almighty, and even language (Medu Neter) was defined as 'Divine Speech'.

Another bonus of supplementary education is that the costs are relatively minimal. When you consider that most English, Mathematics or Science tutors charge approximately £30 - £40 per hour, the £10 - £35 per day for a supplementary school day is an excellent method of academically and socially supporting your child. Regardless, it is at these supplementary schools where the child can obtain a greater sense of self-worth, where the expectations are higher (and unsurprisingly <u>met</u>), where the spiritual element of education can be replaced (as it has been removed), and where they will be treated with love and respect rather than as an insignificant or disruptive minority.

These supplementary schools take many forms, from SAT or strictly GCSE core subject revision classes, and mentoring schemes to traditional Rites of Passage programmes for young boys and girls (see Appendices). As with primary and secondary school entrance, these schools must be thoroughly critiqued to ensure the appropriate development of your child.

You are not like the majority of your friends. Yes I'm talking to you reading this book right now!

Chances are you have walked into a Black bookshop and picked this up. Or you are at a Pan-African event or festival of some kind. Either way, it is likely you are surrounded by a lot of positive energy and people working very hard in our community trying to make a difference. The majority of people in our community do not come to places like this. In fact most do not know where their local African bookshop is located. What you might not know however, is that they are depending on **you**. They won't mention it unless there's an argument or discussion about giving our children a sense of identity and pride in their history and culture. That's when they start feeling defensive and that's when it comes out.

"Well you go to all these Black things! How come you don't come and teach us something!

And there it is.

They have every right to say it, because this knowledge came with a responsibility. And that responsibility is simple,

Each one, teach one.

Yes, you should have emailed everybody to let them know about the last cultural function you went to whether or not you thought they would be interested. Does the fact that you don't go to church stop your Christian friends sending you power-point presentations attached to emails telling you how much Jesus loves you? Even if you think they are cheesy, you still accept them in the loving spirit in which they were sent. The least you can do is the same for your culture and history. It's not as if sending an email is hard work!

You should be telling your friends about good books that you read as a child that you found enjoyable as well as culturally educational.

You should be taking a picture on your phone of that poster you saw in a shop window that had a positive image of an African man. Then, you should send it to your friends who are raising boys and suggest that they have art like that decorating their home. And if the shop is Black-owned, buy one as a gift and pass on the love.

You should be spreading the word about those good films that didn't get much attention, but have strong messages of morality, and justice and spirituality. Things that Hollywood chooses not to provide. We need to support our West African film industry. Some of them may look amateur-quality but trust me, for riveting storylines and powerful messages, they need to be seen. Ask a Nigerian friend for just one or two classics and you'll be hooked! We should keep each other informed of new Black film releases and go to the cinema to watch them during their first week of release. The length of time a cinema screens a film is largely based on the first week's ticket sales,

When you see the Pearls of History Calendars, Posters, Flash Cards, diaries or t-shirts, you should not think about whether **you** need one. You should be thinking about all the friends and family who don't come to places like this. Do they need some? Because whether they have said so or not,

They are depending on you for cultural guidance, support and resources.

The task of educating our children in an inhospitable environment is by definition a difficult one. Do not step lightly. We have an entire generation counting on us!

93

Part 6

Resources & References

You may have realised that your child is not meeting the academic targets that you have set for them. You may have also noticed that within your child's classes or perhaps in their year-group, a significant number of Black children are under-achieving. There is no '**0800**' number for you to call for cultural support. There are no products you can buy on special offer at your local Tesco. You will receive no guidance on the **Lifestyle Channel** because they do not talk about your lifestyle.

The best place for you to find support is at a Black bookshop. Frankly, if you want anything of a cultural nature, or just something constructive for your child to do next weekend your first stop should be the 'flyers' table at your local Black book-shop. I guarantee that even as you ask the question, "Is there anything that you have to help me on…" the other customers in the shop will stop what they are doing to try and help. That's because community-minded people frequent Black bookshops. People like you whose first priority is to support their family, except they see all Black people as their family. We call ourselves Pan-Africanists.

What has been printed below on the next few pages is a list of some bookshops, mentoring and rites of passage programs and radio stations that you should find useful. At this point I offer my apologies as this is by no means a comprehensive list, especially for those living outside London England. However, this is only the first print-run of this book. Please send us an email to advise us of contacts that we should include on the next print of this book so that we can provide more support.

Bookshops (continued)

London – North	London – East
London – North	**London – East**
Headstart Books and Crafts 25 West Green Road, N15, 5BX Telephone: 0208 802 2838 Email: wboaye@yahoo.co.uk	Muatta Books 58 Clarence Road, Clapton, E5, 8HB Telephone: 07956 134 370 Email: muattabooks@yahoo.co.uk
New Beacon Books 76 Stroud Green Road, N4, 3EN Telephone: 0207 272 4889 www.newbeacon-books.com	**London – South**
London – East	All Eyes on Egypt 25 Brixton Station Road, SW2 Telephone: 0207 978 8321 Email: supremenine@aol.com @
All Eyes on Egypt 42 Balls Pond Road, Dalston, N1 4AP Telephone: 0208 254 6442	Nubian Art Centre 27 Catford Broadway, Catford, SE6, 4SN Telephone: 0208 690 1009
Centerprise Bookshop 136 Kingsland High Street, Dalston, E8, 2NS Telephone: 0207 245 9632 Email: eamevor@centerprisetrust.org.uk	Pempamsie 102 Brixton Hill, Brixton, SW2 Telephone: 0208 6710800 www.pempamsie.co.uk
Maarifa Books 6 Bradbury Street ,Dalston Telephone: 0207 503 0300 www.maarifabooks.com	**London – West** African Books Ltd 3 Galena Road, W6 0LT Telephone:0207 746 3646
Mama Afrika Kulcha Shap 282 High Road, Leyton E10, 5PW Telephone: 0208 539 2154	Books and Images 122 – 126 Kilburn High Street, Kilburn, NW6 Telephone:07956 695 808

Bookshops (continued)

London – West	BRIGHTON
London – West	**BRIGHTON**

London – West

Kwazen Books
Unit 20 Groveglade Shopping Hall,
9-13 The Broadway,
West Ealing, W13 9DA
Telephone: 07946 835 686
Email: kwazenbooks@ginikanwa.com

Liberation Corner
95 Wilesden High Road
Telephone:0207 639 3036

BIRMINGHAM

Concious Equation Bookshop
151 Dudley Road, Edgbaston,
Birmingham, B18,7QY
Telephone: 0800 781 0847

Harriet Tubman Bookshop
27 Grove Lane,
Handsworth, Birmingham,
Telephone: 0121 554 8479

Yemanja-A Window to Afrika
446 Birchfield Road,
Perry Bar, Birmingham, B20 3JQ
Telephone: 0121 344 3744
www.yemanjaonline.com

BRIGHTON

Kenya Books
31 Samdout Avenue,
Brighton, BN1, 6EH
Telephone: 01273556629
info@kenyabooks.com

MANCHESTER

Sankofa
132 Claremont Road,
Moss Side, Manchester, M14 4RT
Telephone: 0161 342 0925

West Indian Cultural Centre
Carmoor Road, Manchester
Telephone : 0161 257 2092

NOTTINGHAM

Kuumba
23 Glenworth Road, Radford,
Nottingham, NG7 5QN
Telephone: 01115 847 7232
or 079522369112

Books (continued)

OXFORD	SURREY
African Books Collective The Jam Factory, 27 Park Street, Oxford, OX1, 1HU Telephnone:01865 726686	Kizala 9a George Street, Croydon, Surrey, CR0 1LA Telephone: 0208 688 2601 www.kizala.co.uk
SURREY	**WOLVERHAMPTON**
Egypt on my Mind 39 High Street, Thornton Heath, CR7, 7JF Telephone: 0208 239 0939	Paul Bogle Resource Centre 11 Shockwell Road, Wolverhampton, WV10 9LX Telephone: 01902 731 123

Publishers / Book Distributers

Bogle-L'Ouverture Press
P.O.Box 2186, London W13 9QZ
Telephone: 0208 579 4920
www.newbeacon-books.com

Pepukayi Distribution Services
58 Carew Road, Tottenham, N17 9BA
Telephone:0208 801 0205

BIS Publications
PO BOX 14918 N17 8WJ
Telephone: 0845 226 4066
www.bispublications.com

RADIO STATIONS

These radio stations broadcast educational debates as well as music. For specific program times please visit www. amennoir.com/index.cfm

Baseline	97.9 FM
Blues	94.2 FM
Choice	96.9 FM
Déjà Vu	92.3 FM
Galaxy	99.5 FM
Genesis	91.6 FM
Juice UK	102.5 FM
Lightning	90.8 FM
Millenium Supreme	99.8 FM
Powerjam	92.0 FM
Sweet	89.4 FM

Mentoring Schemes

100 Black Men Of London	www.100bmol.org.uk
Boyhood To Manhood Foundation	www.usatfbmf.com
John Lynch Afrikan Education Programme	www.jlaep.com

Rites Of Passage Programmes

Origin (Boys)	www.newinitiatives.co.uk	020 7738 5833
Akua (Girls)	www.newinitiatives.co.uk	020 7738 5833

Use Of Adinkra Symbols In This Book

The use of symbolism has a long-standing tradition in African culture. Being of Ghanaian lineage (both parents born in Barbados), it was an obvious way to add extra depth and meaning to this body of work.

Adinkra is the name given to the colourful, hand painted and hand-embroidered cloth used for mourning by the Akan people of Ghana and the Ivory Coast. Traditionally, the cloth and symbols embody poetic messages, proverbs and sentiments to express the wearer's feelings about the deceased.

Today, commercial adinkra cloth is worn for all occasions and as everyday clothing. It has now become an important cultural export from Ghana to the rest of the world. It is in this fashion that I have respectfully employed its use.

The use of the Adinkra symbols in this book has not been done randomly. Every attempt has been made to reflect the section of the book being discussed as shown below.

"Except God, I fear none."
Gye Nyame is revered as one of the highest Akan symbols.

This Adinkra symbol has been used first because of its status but also because as parents, you should always have confidence in your ability to do things. The media portrayal of Black youth has always been as an element of society that should be feared. This message carried in this powerful Adinkra symbol not only sets the tone for the rest of the book, but the task that lays before us as a community.

"We learn better out of truth"
This Adinkra symbol is a warning against deception and hypocrisy.

For the section of the book titled "Dispelling Some Myths", this seemed the most appropriate because the motives of all those involved in the educating of our children must be addressed. Once these truths are known, sound judgements can be made regarding our children's education.

"No child is born with teeth"
This symbol derives from the image of a child's teeth, and is a sign of progress in the child's development.

There is a rapid amount of growth at primary school level. The use of this symbol was to reinforce the notion that at this age, this growth is toward being a positive contributing member of the community.

"I do not boast"
This Adinkra symbol is a warning against an inflated pride or an inflated ego.

Today, many parents are heard to say, "Nobody can tell me how to raise my child!" Yesterday, *everyone* in the community had the right to tell you how to raise your child. Furthermore, they had the right to discipline your child as well. The use of this symbol is a call for parents to return to the community values that worked so well in the past. You do not have to do it yourself.

101

"The War Horn"
This is symbolic image of the Akoben war horn. The sound of the akoben is a battle cry; hence, it is a call to action.

This book was designed to be a manual so that parents can act positively for the benefit of their child. Therefore, the "Improvements" section of this book is not just meant to be "a good read", it is where the real work begins.

"The Measuring Rod"
The searching rod, measuring rod or ruler symbolizes perfection.

Whilst looking for educational "Solutions & Models for Success" it seemed entirely appropriate to use a symbol which instructs us to measure our goals against the highest of standards.

"Sew It In Readiness"
This Adinkra symbol demands that we 'be prepared'.

The importance of preparation cannot be overstated. At the Alkebu-Lan Academy Of Excellence, students are taught "Success is 90% preparation and 10% genius. Although this Adinkra symbol also speaks to an individual's resolve, courage and spirit, the need for readiness and foresight is just as important. Hopefully, it will encourage the reader to stand up once the book is put down.

For more information on Adinkra symbols, read the outstanding book, **The Adinkra Dictionary** by W. Bruce Willis

Keep loving your friends,
treasuring your family,
praising creation and
counting your blessings

- it tends to keep everything else in perspective!

Neil Mayers